3-4-60

3-4-60

A VIEW OF EUROPE, 1932

AN INTERPRETATIVE ESSAY ON SOME WORKINGS OF ECONOMIC NATIONALISM

LONDON: HUMPHREY MILFORD
OXFORD UNIVERSITY PRESS

THE WALTER HINES PAGE SCHOOL OF INTERNATIONAL RELATIONS
THE JOHNS HOPKINS UNIVERSITY

A VIEW OF EUROPE, 1932

AN INTERPRETATIVE ESSAY ON SOME WORKINGS OF ECONOMIC NATIONALISM

PAUL van ZEELAND

BALTIMORE
THE JOHNS HOPKINS PRESS
1933

PRINTED IN THE UNITED STATES OF AMERICA
BY J. H. FURST COMPANY, BALTIMORE, MARYLAND

INTRODUCTORY NOTE

The studies constituting this book have been in preparation since the summer of 1932, in response to an invitation to Mr. van Zeeland to deliver a series of lectures at the Johns Hopkins University under the auspices of the Page School of International Relations; and they were completed and forwarded early in April of this year, on the eve of his sailing for the purpose of delivering the lectures at the end of that month and the beginning of May.

In the economic disaster that has overtaken the world, its peoples have been like the survivors of a shipwreck struggling to save themselves by clambering aboard a life-raft too small to bear them, although it might well suffice to float them all to safety if they could subdue their panic and be content merely to cling to it in order to keep their heads above water.

It is plain enough to all of us, at least so far as concerns others, that what requires to be done is not an impossibility or an exaction beyond proportion to the emergency. But in our distress and our bewilderment, we have need of a calm and reassuring voice to bring home to each of us the realization that our own salvation lies in coordinating our action with that of others for the purpose of meeting the common danger.

Mr. van Zeeland, in this study of the workings of economic nationalism, speaks with such a voice—realistically and impartially, with that confident poise that can be gained only from actual experience. For in his capacity as Director of the National Bank of Belgium, as a Deputy Director of the Bank for International Settlements, and as an official representative of the Belgian Government at the various international economic conferences of recent years, he has, in a peculiar sense, lived through both the harsh realities of the crisis and the hopes and the strivings for victory over it. He is therefore able to set forth facts, and to formulate judgments on his

v

observations, with the simplicity and the definiteness of intimate knowledge.

With some background of American university training, he presents his observations in a form congenial to our mode of thinking, even though scrupulously limiting his comments to what he would wish to say to the whole world rather than to our people in particular.

JOHN V. A. MACMURRAY.

THE WALTER HINES PAGE SCHOOL
OF INTERNATIONAL RELATIONS,
MAY 22, 1933.

CONTENTS

A VIEW OF EUROPE, 1932

PART I
INTRODUCTION

CHAPTER I

THE CRISIS AND THE MOVEMENT OF GOODS

The year 1932 has come to an end in a state of utter confusion, both political and economic. The trouble of mind which leaves the select few, no less than the masses, without guidance in the face of accumulated difficulties has already lasted for years. But it has now attained its climax.

Its origin should be traced back to the Great War itself. We are living through one of the last reactions of a shock which has shaken the world to its foundations. But the more direct reasons are to be found as well in the errors of peace as in the consequences of the war.

From the economic point of view, the present crisis is without doubt one of those periodic recessions which enter into the cycle of business. Doubtless no crisis altogether resembles any other; and this one, even apart from its extreme violence, differs in many respects from those which have gone before. Among its characteristics, we shall point out only a few, seeking to put into relief those which have particularly affected Europe.

In following this method, let us nevertheless repeat, in order to avoid any confusion, that the European crisis is intimately bound up with the world crisis, of which it is only a particular manifestation; and furthermore, let us not lose sight of the fact that many of the difficulties, upon which the crisis casts a harsh light, arise out of the necessary evolution of the capitalist regime; they would have presented themselves to us, even without the war, and even without the crisis, though in a weaker form, and under conditions more fitted to allow of a solution.

Section I. The post-war transformation.

It is not our purpose to seek out once more, as has so often been done, the causes of the crisis. We will therefore not set forth the mistakes made amid the beguilements of

1

prosperity, the wild upward swirl of prices, the over-capitalization of enterprises, the premature and/or ill-calculated transformations in the organization of production. But in the growing paralysis which is creeping over us everywhere, we will endeavor to set into relief the mistakes and the changes which have affected the mechanism of the distribution of goods throughout the world. We will particularly dwell upon the financial aspect of this mechanism, and upon its dislocations. In thus emphasizing the aspect of the crisis which concerns the movement of goods, we think that we are touching upon a point which, with the passing of time, has become fundamental. Whatever may have been the remote origins of the crisis, it is practically certain that it would never have attained such a degree of depth and of seriousness if, for whatever reason or under whatever influence, men had not, by blundering and ill-conceived interventions blocked more and more the movements of goods and of capital.

Let us go back to before the war. In those days, as the story goes, harmony, equilibrium and plenty prevailed. International economic relations had attained a degree of stability and of regularity sufficient to permit their development. This state of affairs furthermore favored a corresponding degree of equilibrium within most countries.

From the commercial point of view, it was characterized by the permanency—relative, but sufficient—of the rôle played by the different markets and of the direction taken by the great currents of trade. From this point of view, one cannot too much insist upon the importance, for the effective, prompt and easy distribution of goods, of those traditions, habits, personal relationships, prejudices and facilities, which make up the currents of trade.

But it was especially in the field of finance that order made itself felt before the war. Certain great centers—London, Paris, Berlin, Vienna—supported by others less powerful but as well managed, assured the satisfaction of the many and various needs for capital. One served principally as the distributor of long-term capital. Another played the rôle of a general intermediary for one or another part of Europe.

The currencies of the principal states, solidly based on gold, were so stable, and for so long a time, that the great mass of people no longer remembered monetary troubles.

Lastly and especially, these different needs, and these services rendered to production at all stages, rested upon an enormous and active reservoir of capital — London. This market played the essential rôle; it exercised that " marginal influence " whose importance is decisive. Admirably organized, strong in knowledge and in traditions proved twenty times over, able to keep its head in times of difficulty and to help others even by assuming for itself an excess of risk, organized to respond to the infinite diversity of the needs of international commerce,—the market of the City was in truth the masterpiece of an incomparable and delicate mechanism for the distribution of products throughout the world.

In short, international monetary stability, harmony between the needs of capital and the resources available, harmony among the different classes of capital, whether short-term or long- term, strength and firmness on the part of lenders capable of following and of aiding borrowers in their many needs, —such is, in outline, the financial picture of before the war.

To be sure, this picture should not be painted in too rosy colors. Difficulties were not lacking even then, and an attentive observer could discover the germs of more than one of our present miseries. But all in all, and with the necessary reservations, the situation presented in very large degree the characteristics that we have pointed out.

To what has been said let us add one thing that is fundamental and yet often left out of consideration. The world was divided, obviously, into two groups—the creditor countries, and the debtor countries. Now, the creditors took the attitude that common sense and their own interest dictated to them: they were, permanently, givers of capital and takers of goods; in other words, the markets of the creditor countries gave out, in the form of loans, a part of the excess of their balance of payments; they absorbed the difference in the form of imports of merchandise, which led to a constant deficit in

2

their commercial balance. That was a condition *sine qua non* of the continuity of the international movement of trade.

    *   *   *   *   *   *

As against the picture of before the war, let us now set up that of since the war. The change is striking. It can be summed up in the phrase, upsetting of equilibrium.

From the economic point of view, the traditional positions are overthrown. Throughout Europe, currents of trade that had for long been stable have been brusquely interrupted.

Let us take two examples. The three sections of the old Poland had economic relations in three distinct or opposed directions; after the reconstitution of the nation, these economic currents had to be turned back and reorganized in order to find the necessary unity. A deep patriotism and an energetic will assured success, but at the price of strenuous efforts and many sacrifices.

In Central Europe, the Austro-Hungarian monarchy had, whether by the extent of its frontiers or by the attraction of its power, achieved in fact a Danubian economy; its crumbling deflected the flow of a thousand and one traditional currents, which have not yet been able to form again.

No doubt, the forces and the needs in which these commercial currents have their origin have not disappeared. In the end, they find their ways; but not indeed without trouble, delay and effort.

The general readjustment of after the war, which would have been troublesome under any circumstances, was made still more complicated by the political difficulties, the violent hatreds, the contradictions of all sorts that followed from the remaking of the map of Europe. The accentuation of economic nationalism has retarded if not indeed prevented this readjustment in many cases; and one may say that the greater part of the task still remains to be accomplished.

A similar displacement of the centers of equilibrium is to be observed in the industrial domain. The war favored the establishment of powerful instruments of production in the new countries, or at any rate in those newly developing industry. Let us only recall the profound transformation undergone by the textile industry in consequence of the industrial developments in Asia.

But it is in the realm of finance that the change has shown itself most profound and most unfortunate.

One fact, to begin with, dominates the whole problem: it is that the war has transformed into creditors countries that had hitherto been debtors, and *vice versa.* Other countries, moreover, while remaining creditors on final account, have seen the credit side of their balance reduced in very considerable proportion.

In the field of currency, there was to begin with a long period of increasing depreciation, and of infinite variations, which ended in the series of definitive devalorizations. One of the permanent effects of these troubles consists in the dispersal and in the destruction of an important part of the capital at the disposal of any national economy.

There is another effect, almost as serious: it is the persistence, in public opinion, of a profound distrust in regard to permanent investments as expressed in monetary units. This psychological element has weighed heavily upon the development of events.

As to the international mechanism for the distribution of credit, it was upset even in its essential parts. Certain great traditional markets were excluded, whether for a prolonged time, like Berlin and Vienna, or for the period of monetary instability, like Paris. But the greatest misfortune was the setback of the London market, and its incapacity to carry out fully its essential rôle as a central reservoir and as an intermediary between the demand and the supply of capital in its various forms.

Immediately after the war, London no doubt suffered from the depreciation of the pound in relation to gold. But the prestige of the English currency remained always intact; by comparison with other moneys, with the exception of the dollar, its solidity and relative stability seemed worthy of envy. No one doubted that it would regain its ancient gold parity. The English leaders were conscious of London's financial rôle

in the world. It seemed to impose upon them a duty which
was consonant with their own interest. The pound was reestablished at its gold parity in 1925. It may be said that it was
not this temporary curve in the quotation of the pound that
actually weakened London.

But before the war, the financial predominance of England
rested upon two principal pillars—on the one hand, a very
heavy credit excess in its balance of payments, and on the
other, a considerable part in international commerce itself.
Now, both found themselves diminished and weakened; in
particular, England's part in international commerce, either
in absolute or in relative figures, has been so reduced that
there is no longer a question of preponderance.

London was therefore obliged, by the mere force of circumstances, to limit its participation in the various fields of
international finance.

But the place thus left empty was not, alas, occupied either
completely or adequately by anyone.

Other markets doubtless increased their effort. Holland
and Switzerland saw their relative importance very largely
increased; but their resources are too limited for them to be
able to exercise an important effect upon world forces. Two
other great markets intervened: these were New York, at
first, and then Paris, after the return of the franc to a gold
basis.

Let us frankly recognize the fact: New York would have
been able, after the war, to assume in international financing
a rôle analogous to that formerly played by London, and to
take the very first place. The material elements were all to
be found gathered in the hands of the United States: large
creditors as they were, very rich, exalted by victory, and with
their currency intact, they lacked nothing.

But international financing is, in all its parts, a dangerous
ground, full of pitfalls. To succeed in it, there are needed a
profound knowledge of the markets, a great diversity of services and an even greater capacity for adaptation, long traditions, large reserves, much composure, and sometimes great
patience. These exceptional qualities are rare. Even when

found together, they do not suffice; they must also be developed in a favorable atmosphere.

Certainly both places, New York and Paris, seized their opportunity courageously. Strong individualities were revealed. Partial efforts were crowned with success. To tell the truth, the action of New York and that of Paris even surpassed what could reasonably have been expected of them by anyone familiar with the difficulties of the task and of the rôle.

But making all allowances, the gap was not at all filled. Paris soon limited itself almost exclusively to long-term and stock exchange operations. New York worked fitfully, sometimes nervously, and displaying brusque changes of attitude. Neither in France nor in the United States was there created the " favorable atmosphere " which would no doubt have resulted from an adequate economic policy and in particular from a liberal commercial policy.

They lacked, moreover, one of the essential supports, necessary to the playing of this rôle—a broad and flexible tariff policy, assuring an active and diversified trade as regards importation no less than exportation.

* * * * * *

Let us take our bearings at the moment when prosperity was at its height, about 1928-29.

The normal proportion among the different categories of credits was deranged. In the total of capital loaned, that which took the form of short-term operations was by far the greater part; investment capital, which could and should have been put out on long terms, remained mobile. That was the fruit of the general distrust that monetary troubles and political instability had engendered.

But just laws cannot be violated with impunity.

The need for long-term credits existed. In the absence of long-term capital, it was satisfied by the immobilization of funds borrowed on short term, through operations indefinitely renewed. There followed a hidden but serious disorder: the dislocation of maturity dates, the lack of synchronism in debit and credit operations, the incompatibility between obligations and facts.

This situation was made still more grave, from the international point of view, by the profound difference in the situations in the lending and the borrowing countries.

With the lenders, there was a superabundance of short-term funds, favored by the abuses and errors in the practice of the gold exchange standard. With many of the borrowers, on the contrary, there was a diminution or even a practical disappearance of the circulating capital due to inflation and to the flight of capital which is the inevitable result of it. The abuses were concealed under genuine international needs which justified a certain number of operations.

To top it all, a general fever of investment, and a collective tendency towards the extension of equipment, led to enormous mistakes in over-capitalization—mistakes that had to be paid for in any case but which took on a much more serious character when they were accompanied by an immobilization of funds borrowed on short term.

Stock market speculation followed a similar course, and seemed limitless. The bourses of Europe and America were rivals in a race which seemed to be both an endurance race and a sprinting race.

Surely, there were warnings to be heard. But with what complacency they were ignored!

Ingenious theories had been worked out to justify this movement, whose continuous upward tendency seemed to be without precedent. I recall one original attempt at explanation: the technical perfection of the instruments of production and of the means of distribution of goods must have as its result the lowering of the proportional yield on shares; the rate of capitalization of stocks should be lowered; at the same time, it was considered legitimate to borrow at higher rates than formerly, the real return and the capital profits serving as more than a sufficient counterweight. This queer reasoning was applied especially to the American market and I have heard it preached in London as late as 1929.

Another general mistake, attributable no less to the borrowers than to the lenders, had been committed in the final stages of the boom: that was the exaggeration of interest rates.

When one considers an isolated credit operation, even if it is a very large one, it is possible to justify a very high rate of interest. There are undertakings which realize enormous profits and which can in consequence bear a heavy debt service. When, moreover, an isolated case is involved, an error of judgment does not always result tragically; supposing that the debtor does not make enough to pay both the interest and the amortization of the debt, the creditor still has a chance to get back his capital from the assets of the undertaking.

But the whole question appears in a different light when it concerns a vast economic unity—an entire branch of industry, for example, or a country. In this case, a mass foreclosure of defaulting debtors is impossible. In order that the obligations incidental to the debt (that is to say, interest and amortization) should be kept up, they must be assured by actual gains—by increases in the wealth of the debtor. The principal element of appreciation therefore lies in the average return of the industry in question, or of the whole organization of production in the country in question.

We have available statistics for a sufficient time, giving us indications of this sort; and there are some of them especially which permit a measurement of the average net return on capital invested in a group of industries; and none of them reaches an average of five per cent. This figure might no doubt be increased for new countries; but it may be kept, for the purposes of an indication, and with the usual reserves, to furnish a basis for a judgment where economically developed countries are concerned.

So, then, when a country finds itself burdened with a large foreign debt, and this debt has been contracted at very high interest rates, there is no reason to be astonished if the possibility of paying comes into question, sooner or later. A precise opinion in this or that case is doubtless always difficult to reach; a thousand considerations come into play; the argument only applies if the debt is of such size as to make it comparable with the total of the debtor's revenues; moreover, an average must be established for the various classes of borrowed funds; and finally, it must be remembered that an average is never a reality, but a more or less artificial indication by which to arrive at it.

It nevertheless remains the fact that certain countries of Europe had contracted considerable debts on conditions such that the service of them (interest and amortization) exceeded, even in that epoch of prosperity, their regular capacity to earn. These excessive obligations were undertaken at the moment of the dizzy height of prices. The lowering of prices which has since taken place has greatly increased the real burden of this debt. The crisis has reduced at the same time the volume of production and the value in monetary units of this reduced production; while the obligations remain fixed at their nominal level.

The break became inevitable.

And finally—last but not least—still further encumbering the channels already obstructed by so many economic or financial obstacles, we find the payments of reparations and inter-allied debts.

Arising out of political obligations, representing the service of capital destroyed by the war, such payments must, on whatever hypothesis, weigh heavily upon the world. I do not say that they were impossible. They might have been carried out. But in order that that might be done, they would have had to be led into, lost, and mingled in a vast and genuine movement of material progress, in a world more open, more united and more reasonable than ever before; the creditors would have had to consent to be paid in the only possible means of payment—that is, in merchandise and services.

To a vigorous organism, a slight excess is not crippling. Upon an organism that is fevered and shaken, the least shock has tragic consequences. In the conditions that prevailed in Europe in 1928, as we have just described them, it goes without saying that the international political payments could not but exert a disproportionate and disastrous influence.

Section II. The emergence of the monetary difficulties.

The pendulum of the crises had come to the highest point of its swing. The shock of a swing backwards could not but be formidable. It affected in the first place the markets for raw materials and the bourses. The decline of prices, the Wall Street crash in 1929, and the breakdown of security values in the entire world should have opened all eyes to the depth and intensity of the movement which was beginning. But a heroic courage would have been needed at that moment to measure coolly the extent of the damage and to consent to the necessary sacrifices. It was easier to nourish illusions, to try to keep prosperity by such words as "confidence, courage, an interval, etc.", which today seem to us vain and crude. Behind this veil, events continued their march.

The profound weakening that the continuous decline in raw materials and in securities had inflicted upon the economy of the world became manifest only in 1931, when the crisis broke forth afresh in a cascade of financial catastrophes.

As often happens in such cases, it was a local event, in itself of limited importance, which started the movement—the downfall, in May, 1931, of one of the oldest and most respectable banking establishments of the Continent, the *Oesterreichische Kreditanstalt,* at Vienna.

This event was only an occasion, rather than a cause. The fruit was ripe, and would have fallen anyhow. But this constitutes in fact the first link in a long chain. The reasons that led to the downfall of the *Kreditanstalt* are likewise to be found, in their main lines, in the other banking or financial catastrophes that followed one after the other. For this reason, therefore, we shall, by way of illustration, make some further analysis of it.

The policy of the institution in the matter of credit and investment was marked by that craze which led the majority of the banks of Europe and indeed of the world to unjustifiable excesses in the immobilization of funds in industry.

This error, serious everywhere, was disastrous in Austria because the economic position of the country is extremely weak and difficult. Reduced to a few millions of inhabitants,

isolated from its traditional *hinterland,* the Austrian state
seems scarcely workable. A splendid city, Vienna, is stran-
gled within frontiers that are too narrow—a head without a
body. To reestablish a permanent equilibrium, there would
have had to be in Austria a profound effort towards readjustment and adaptation. But two conditions were necessary for
success—a powerful movement of national opinion, and
relations with the rest of Europe on a reasonable basis: and
both were lacking.

Austrian opinion has never rallied from the defeat. The
new constitution is itself a factor of disunity. Upon a small
country, crushed and divided against itself, the attraction of
a great neighbor of the same language and the same race,
Germany, could not fail to have a preponderant influence.
The economic union that the Protocol of March 19, 1931,
would have established between the two countries was a
scarcely disguised form of *Anschluss*; the Permanent Court
of International Justice at the Hague declared, in its con-
sultative opinion of September 5, 1931, that the measure was
in contradiction to the international engagements undertaken
by Austria, and the project was not carried forward. The
rapprochement is nevertheless being followed out, step by
step, through the progressive unification of numerous
details of political and economic life, assured by identical
decisions taken side by side in Austria and in Germany.

It goes without saying that the loans made to an industry
that was hypertrophied, over-capitalized, weighted with social
charges, working in such an atmosphere of abandon and of
political *laissez-aller,* could not easily be recovered.

Moreover, the *Kreditanstalt* had suffered, in various forms,
from arbitrary or excessive interventions of the state, either
in its own affairs, or in the economic and social life of the
country.

In October, 1929, it had been practically compelled, by an
intense political pressure, to take over the *Boden Kreditanstalt,* a land loan institution which was in difficulties. This
merger was unjustifiable from the purely banking point of
view, and contributed largely to weakening the *Kreditanstalt.*

Moreover, the whole Austrian economy is weighted down by social laws which assure considerable advantages to the laboring classes, but which establish throughout the country a scale of living in excess of its normal capacity. Certain of these laws affect particularly the banks. There was one of them, which was maintained up to 1933, which practically guaranteed to employees stability of employment and of salary. The result was that, even in a time of general or particular crisis, an establishment found it in fact impossible to reduce its general expenses. This was notably true of the *Kreditanstalt*.

The institution therefore found itself, behind an unbroken façade, emptied of a great part of its substance. When the façade itself crumbled, events began to occur. But the *Kreditanstalt* occupied so preponderant a place in Austrian economy that its abrupt disappearance would have carried away with it into the abyss the bulk of the industry of Austria. The public authorities therefore intervened and, little by little, found themselves completely involved.

The first unfavorable rumors had their usual consequence: the depositors, both nationals and foreigners, began to withdraw their funds. The National Bank of Austria energetically supported the *Kreditanstalt*. When the normal portfolio was exhausted, it discounted for it emergency paper—notes which mobilized the more or less secure credits of the *Kreditanstalt* to Austrian industry. Its portfolio of commerical paper, between April 30, 1931, and December 31, 1931, increased from 89,000,000 shillings to 908,000,000 shillings. It was thus possible to meet the withdrawals and to avoid, at least for the time being, a domestic moratorium.

But foreign depositors withdrew their funds not only from the *Kreditanstalt*; they withdrew them from Austria. Besides, the Austrians themselves, feeling the storm approaching, and keeping vivid memories of the monetary collapse of 1919-23, likewise sought shelter abroad. There was brought about a violent movement of capital, which had the effect of rapidly exhausting the reserves in gold and foreign monies of the Central Bank.

Believing it still possible to ride the storm, the Government and the National Bank asked for support abroad. The Bank for International Settlements and, under its aegis, a group of central banks, lent the National Bank of Austria large sums which the latter added to its metallic reserve. These new reserves were exhausted with equal rapidity. The gold and currency reserves, which amounted to 929,000,000 shillings (say $131,000,000) at the end of December, 1930, were reduced to 317,000,000 shillings (say $44,000,000) at the end of 1931, and to 192,000,000, shillings (say $27,000,-000) at the end of June, 1932, in spite of short-term loans of 190,000,000 shillings granted by the Bank for International Settlements and the Bank of England; Austria therefore soon found itself confronting the same difficulty as before.

Here is the dilemma which was presented to her—either to suspend the convertibility of notes into gold or foreign currency, abandon the exchange market to its fate, and allow the general readjustment to take place of itself, whatever might be the consequences, or else to maintain at any cost the gold level of the currency, by artificially restraining the movements of capital which might influence it.

The choice was difficult. In the first hypothesis, the currency was sacrificed. The second hypothesis compromised the credit of the country, and thrust it onto a down grade of which none could perceive the end, and with nothing less sure than its success.

Nevertheless, Austria did not hesitate; she chose the second. To understand this attitude, one must enter into the state of mind of people who have lived through the tortures of inflation, who have experienced the terrible effects of a total monetary depreciation, and who still suffer from the scarcely healed wounds due to the last crisis of the sort. It is quite possible that the social organism could not have endured, at so short an interval, a repetition of such a shock, and would have found itself anew under the direct menace of a complete collapse.

Without doubt, the monetary conditions were quite different. In 1919-23, the cause of the inflation lay in the un-balance of public finance and the printing of paper money for the state's account. That was no longer the case in 1931; the budget being balanced, the depreciation upon the exchange market would soon have found a natural limit.

But to this objection the Austrians made a double answer. A monetary depreciation, even moderate, involved the risk of bringing about an internal unbalance of the budget, which might have thrust them again into the vicious circle of the years 1919-23. They had, moreover, to reckon with the reactions of a public opinion which was nervous and distressed, and which a monetary movement, even though moderate at the beginning, might have made completely panicky.

It was for these reasons that Austria entered upon the way of a foreign moratorium and of exchange regulations.

*   *   *   *   *   *

But Vienna had continued to play a rôle in the financing of Central and Eastern Europe. The blocking of funds directly affected a number of small states. Furthermore, the example created anxiety. Those foreigners who possessed large funds in Central Europe took fright. The panic extended to the nationals. An abrupt and violent exodus of capital towards several countries of refuge, such as the United United States and France, shook Central and Eastern Europe.

Meanwhile, there brutally intervened a number of influences that had not been felt up to this time. The checking of speculation in Wall Street and the progressive tightening up of funds in the United States, due to more and more frequent losses, exercised a double effect upon the financial situation of Europe; the abundant and continuous flow of American loans was suddenly absolutely interrupted, driving a whole series of states from the habits of excessive plenty and plunging them brusquely into penury; and at the same time, the American capitalists and bankers, rightly apprehending the most serious difficulties, themselves called for the wholesale repayment of their short-term loans.

After striking Austria, the blow struck Germany with a

double violence. Confronting the same dilemma, she resolved it in the same way, sacrificing for the sake of monetary stability her international credit and the prestige of her great banks.

But it is manifest that the default of a country like Germany, which occupies a considerable place in the economy of Europe, must carry with it profound consequences.

The most serious effect of all was that upon London. An identical exodus of capital soon led England herself to deal with the dilemma; but she chose the opposite course. On September 21, 1931, the world learned with stupefaction that the pound sterling and gold had taken separate ways.

England's decision was imitated by a series of countries— Sweden, Denmark, Portugal, Egypt, Finland, Ireland, Greece, etc. The storm blew even further. It reached the United States, it touched Holland and Switzerland, and barely touched Belgium. But in those countries, the resistence was successful.

Thus it was that Europe entered the year of misfortune, 1932: of the thirty-odd countries that make up Europe, ten had explicitly suspended the gold standard; a dozen, such as Albania, Austria, Bulgaria, Hungary, Spain, and Yugoslavia, etc., encased in a triple armor of restrictions of every sort, had legal or actual bans or regulations upon the traffic in currency; a half-dozen only—for example, France, Belgium, Holland and Switzerland—still applied with sufficient flexibility the rules of the gold standard.

PART II

THE STRUGGLE AGAINST THE CRISIS,
AND ITS DEFEAT

CHAPTER II

THE MEASURES OF ECONOMIC NATIONALISM

We are, then, confronting an intense economic crisis, marked by a tremendous fall in prices. At a critical moment of its development, it is thrust back upon the slope to the abyss by an exceptional credit crisis, which at once gives rise to a grave monetary crisis.

The obvious characteristic of this whole crisis is its universality; from beginning to end it bears the clearest indications of its international character. No country escapes it, whatever may be its political or its economic system. Many are drawn into the circle less, perhaps, by their own mistakes than by the events or the reactions brought to bear on them from outside. Never has the economic interdependence of the world appeared more striking than in this chain of catastrophes.

Now we are witnessing this paradoxical spectacle: each country seems intent upon struggling against the crisis by protecting itself alone and by leaving for its neighbors the sacrifices to be made; each seeks to save itself alone, even to the detriment of the others; in other words, the whole effort of resistance to a specifically international crisis seems to be modeled upon a strictly national plan.

Need it be said that a method so contradictory could not but fail?

We propose to examine in succession several of the means of protection put into operation by states at bay; we will then examine why the international organizations have proved impotent; we will pause a moment at several sporadic efforts towards reaction along international lines, and we will try to strike a summary balance of this long series of failures.

Section I. Protectionism: tariffs, contingents, prohibitions.

All the international conferences which have dealt with the problem, and all the meetings of experts which have

3   19

examined it, have always come to the same conclusion that the accentuation of protectionism is injurious for all nations and for each one of them. Likewise, in economic doctrine, I do not know of any authoritative voice which has been raised in defense of the principle of an extreme national protection.

And meanwhile, with the same unanimity in practice as in theory, but in direct contradiction thereto, the states have not ceased to emphasize unilateral measures designed for the protection of their domestic markets.

Unfortunately there is, in protectionism, an internal logic; it pushes on the state that has recourse to it, constantly further along a way which, even though it be long, no less surely ends in a blind alley. Customs tariffs soon prove insufficient; they are reinforced by narrower and narrower systems of quotas; and these in turn call for more or less openly avowed but radical prohibitions.

In order that a customs tariff may protect a market effectively and continuously, recourse must constantly be had to increases of duties.

As for a general tariff, its average incidence ends by incorporating itself in the general level of prices within the protected country. The period of adaptation varies with the economic structure of the different countries; but in no case is it more than a few years. By the time this has elapsed, the cost of internal production has been increased by a charge corresponding quite closely to the tariff margin. International competition reappears in a relative situation, as regards the national producers, corresponding to that which existed before the establishment of the tariff. There is perhaps one difference which is brought about and which continues, but it works to the disadvantage of the protected country. This is that, during the period of transition, its industry will probably have relaxed the effort necessary to keep it in the very first rank of technique, while competitors (or some of them at any rate), driven by necessity, will have succeeded in improving their conditions of production.

And so, after some time, the reasons which had led to the

establishment of protection in the first place are found again unaltered, or else even strengthened. A stronger pressure is brought to bear in order to obtain a further increase of duties.

The same phenomena go on thus repeating themselves from time to time, to the point of absurdity.

On the other hand, so far as concerns a duty which affects only one product, or several of them, but too few to influence seriously the domestic price level, protection is and may continue to be effective, even if the duty is kept at the same level. It is, in that case, a bounty paid to one category of producers by the whole population. But here, too, the logic of the system tends towards its extension: when an industry finds itself confronted with serious competition, it will be led to claim for itself a special protection such as that which its neighbor enjoys; and step by step, this protection by classes runs the risk of thus extending to the point where its effects will resemble those of a general tariff.

And this is how things went. In 1932 alone, we have counted in Europe 237 modifications or extensions of tariffs, and 71 increases of duties.

But there comes a moment when the raising of duties is ineffective or politically impossible—ineffective, either because economic conditions have been upset to the point of rendering temporarily inoperative all considerations relative to the price of goods, or because it has exhausted all its consequences;—impracticable, either because internal political conditions are unfavorable, or because the stipulations of commercial treaties are explicitly opposed.

*   *   *   *   *   *

Protectionism then makes appeal to the system of quotas. The method consists in opening the frontiers to strictly limited quantities of goods, and closing them as soon as these contingents have been reached.

It may be applied in very different degrees. As bearing upon certain rare products, and fixing for them quotas approximating a habitual movement in these branches of commerce, it seems at first sight harmless enough.

Even in this first degree, however, it lends itself to very serious criticism. In fact, the fixation of a commercial tendency at a certain moment of its development is always an arbitrary act; it introduces, in a domain where mobility and flexibility are requisite, a hardening which acts as harmfully as a foreign body in a living organism; and it should be added that in practice, such provisions, nine times out of ten, favor (to a degree not justified by any service rendered) narrow private interests—notably those of certain intermediaries enjoying an established position.

But it is rare that the partisans of this method stop at this first degree. Carried on by the inescapable dynamics of protectionism, they go on step by step to a point at which the system condemns itself. The list of goods subject to contingents is indefinitely extended, and bears upon products such as brooms, meat-choppers or picture-books, to which it is difficult to attach any general interest. Moreover, the size of the contingents is more and more reduced, and leads to an actual exclusion.

The method has been still further perfected, so to speak, in certain countries. Instead of being fixed by the year, the contingents have been for shorter and shorter periods, some of them now varying from month to month. It is not necessary to have a long practical experience to realize that, under such conditions, trade becomes a gamble. Whether or not the contingents are accompanied by licenses, the effect is the same; the only difference is in a secondary mode of their application.

*   *   *   *   *   *

Beyond this point, there remains for protectionism no further weapon unless it be complete prohibition. But let us not forget that protectionism is almost always ashamed of itself; it is forever seeking to disguise itself, it invokes the best reasons in the world, and it finds a thousand pretexts to justify its attitudes one after the other. Reaching the limit of its development in the prohibition of entry of goods, it is still insincere. It is for that reason that many measures which are in reality absolute exclusions take the disguise of other decisions.

It is clear that, for example, when a customs duty exceeds by 700% the value of the product, it is no longer a matter of tariff provisions, but in fact a disguised prohibition. Likewise, when a contingent is so narrow that it lowers by 95% the trade in a product, it amounts practically to a closing of the frontier.

There are measures legitimate in themselves which are applied in such a spirit that they become unquestionable prohibitions. Thus under the pretext of hygiene, of protection against animal or plant diseases, there are cases in which all trade in certain animal or vegetable products has been completely excluded for years at a time. And let us here make mental note of the use that has been made of measures designed in the first instance to protect the currency, and which have involved extensive prohibitions. We will have occasion to refer to them later.

*   *   *   *   *   *

But in Europe, even less than in the rest of the world, the states were not economically isolated before the crisis; they were bound together by a network of treaties of commerce; the most-favored-nation clause had become general and had in fact tightened up the meshes. How was it that the wave of protectionism was not broken against it?

We must acknowledge it, foregoing a large share of our pride, that if these treaties have not been violated in their letter they have too often been perverted in spirit and evaded in practice. Means have sometimes been employed with which the least that one can reproach them is pettiness. Such is the case of the exaggerated and increasing specification of goods in tariffs. We have emphasized how unfairly certain clauses looking to the protection of health have been applied; is not that doing violence to the goodwill of the other party?

Even more often, it is by measures listed under the caption " monetary " that the obligations of the treaties have been escaped.

And finally, many occasions for denunciation have been

seized. The agreements which have replaced the previous treaties have taken on a striking character of instability and of tentativeness. They are rather *modus vivendi* than real treaties. And when, moreover, the duration of an agreement depends on one of the parties, when either can put an end to it at will by means of notification a few days in advance, can one still speak of treaties? Nothing remains of them but the appearance. All stability has gone. Each contracting party really keeps its elbow room free and is in a position to adapt its commercial policy to immediate necessities or changing circumstances, without regard for its partners. Under such conditions, do not international commercial relations rest upon shifting sands?

The months that have just gone by have accentuated the evil; great countries like England, France, Germany, etc., have taken even more definitely an attitude of withdrawal into themselves. We may cite, among other cases since the Ottawa agreements, the *avenant* to the German-French Treaty of Commerce (December, 1932), and the recent German-Swiss Treaty (November, 1932). Countries, like Portugal and Rumania, have newly had recourse to the régime of restrictions, while others have increased them. And meanwhile, the slump in business has become deeper and deeper.

Section II.   Exchange regulations.

There are few countries which have not, in various degrees, had recourse to the preceding methods of protectionism. But only the strongest of them have been able to limit themselves to these. Elsewhere, reaction to the crisis, following always a narrowly national spirit, has taken on other aspects even more radical and charged with grave consequences for the future of international relations.

Throughout all one part of Europe, this reaction took the form of monetary depreciation. Doubtless there is no question here of an attitude freely chosen, and adopted after mature deliberation by those interested. In the majority of cases, the abandonment of the gold standard was, at a given moment, an implacable necessity.

However that may be, many currencies are found today without any common basis. Each follows its own course. Those which have been dragged down by the fall of the pound sterling find themselves, for the most part, separated from the pound as well as from gold.

The variability of depreciated currencies in relation to gold currencies, like that of the depreciated currencies in relation to one another, introduces into international relations an additional element of trouble and uncertainty, so obvious and so well known that it would be superfluous to insist upon it.

A single fact will make clear the depth of the possible consequences: very serious lowering of the pound sterling with relation to gold has each time led to an accentuation of the lowering of gold prices, thus making the crisis harder and more difficult to resolve for the whole world.

Let us, in passing, recall the courageous attitude that England took in 1923-25 in the face of the monetary crisis which was then shaking Europe. She unceasingly emphasized the dangers that the disorder of the exchanges presented for the community of nations—for the countries with strong currency no less than for those whose currency was weakened. She took the lead in most of the movements for recovery, and continually lent her support and her resources to every effort tending to restore the European currencies to a common and stable basis.

*   *   *   *   *   *

Like the countries which have suspended the gold standard, those which have surrounded themselves with strict exchange regulations have acted under the pressure of forces that, at a given moment, were often inescapable. They had to choose not between regulation and liberty, but between regulation and the fall of their currency.

Let us examine the terms of the problems with which they were confronted.

Capital, fleeing from the country, seeks refuge abroad. The reserves of currency and of gold of the central bank are depleted. In a final effort, these are restored by short-term borrowings of foreign monies. The effort is in vain: the movement continues. One step more, and the central bank must confess itself defeated; the currency must be abandoned to its fate.

This step, one group of countries refused to take—for instance Austria, Germany and Hungary. To protect the remnant of the gold cover, the currents that are carrying capital abroad must be stopped. They are many; some of the principal ones are these—service of the long-term foreign debt (amortization and interest); payment of interest upon the short-term foreign debt, and especially the wholesale and hurried repayment of principal of this debt; the payment for imports of merchandise; speculative sales against foreign currency on the part of panic-stricken investors or of specialists, on the lookout for an exchange profit.

In this list, certain elements, like the regular service of foreign debts, appear as customary items of the balance of payments; others, such as hurried short-term repayments, and the flight of capital, as exceptional elements. No country, however strong, could stand the abrupt withdrawal of a large quantity of short-term capital, or resist the general and persistent lack of confidence of the mass of its investors. These elements must all the more affect countries economically weak or weakened by the crisis.

Moreover, the equilibrium of the balance of payments, even when reduced to its normal elements, was in many cases upset by the collapse of prices. The greater part of the countries of Central and Eastern Europe have, to fulfill their foreign engagement—that is to say, to effect the service of their debt and to pay for imports of finished products—only one important resource, the exportation of agricultural products. Now this exportation has been affected by a double diminution because of the crisis—a reduction of total volume of exports through the closing or the contracting of markets, and a diminution of the price of each unit exported.

Every effort of the countries which sought to maintain their currency at the same level has therefore been directed

towards reestablishing a certain equilibrium in the balance
of payments, by struggling, on the one hand, to increase
exports, and, on the other hand, to stop the draining away
of funds.

*   *   *   *   *   *

In all regulations with regard to the sale and the purchase
of foreign currency, we find in the first place a series of
decisions forbidding in the most absolute fashion the movements of capital of a purely speculative or financial character.
No demand for foreign monies is met if it is not justified
by an economic transaction serving as its basis, such, for
example, as the payment for merchandise imported.

But that is only a first step, which necessarily calls for
others. The flight of capital takes a variety of forms. It may
well assume the appearance of an outflow of merchandise;
the flight from the currency, even within the frontiers, often
consists in excessive or hasty purchases of goods, considered
as real and stable values.

Those in control are therefore compelled, by the force of
circumstances, not only to examine whether a demand for
exchange is based upon a commercial operation, but also to
judge this operation itself, and inquire whether or not it is of
a normal and regular character. But what is the criterion of
normality or of regularity? Is it enough that a commercial
operation should exclude all idea of speculation or of the
transfer of capital, in order that it may at once be approved
and be entitled to have foreign currency allowed?

Far from it! There was too good a chance to try to favor
by this means an adjustment of the commercial balance.
Importations were therefore passed through a sieve; some
were continued, as serving the general interests of the country, as, for example, raw materials, semi-finished products, or
indispensable goods; others were refused as superfluous—
luxury products, finished products and competing products.

Such was the logic of facts. To justify these regulations
which became no less commercial than monetary, a variety of
reasons were advanced, and not all of them were bad. A

number of countries could confront their creditors with this dilemma: " We cannot pay you except with a surplus of exports; which do you prefer—that we employ the means suited to create this surplus, or that we stop our payments abroad?" The answer was difficult.

But the system opened the doors to many abuses. It became one of the most brutal and most dangerous forms of protectionism. None allowed a more easy escape from certain burdensome clauses of the commercial treaties.

Sometimes it led to situations of crying injustice. The importation of goods was not itself forbidden, but payment abroad had been made impossible. The foreigner exporting in good faith thus found himself caught in a trap. It is of no use to say that the foreign exporter, if he had been well advised, might have been able to guard against such risk when once the first surprise had occurred. For all these complicated and confused regulations are essentially unstable; their provisions vary almost from day to day at the will of those administering them; their putting into force gives occasion for all sorts of arbitrariness, whether in the granting or refusal of authorizations for currency, or in the establishment of the percentages allowed.

In short, the organization charged with centralizing the operations in foreign exchange becomes the supreme and irresponsible regulator of the intercourse between the interested country and the rest of the world. Was it fitted to fulfill this rôle? One can boldly answer, " No ".

In the majority of cases, it was the central bank which was charged with supervision over the traffic in currency, either directly or through the medium of an agency more or less independent of it. This choice is understandable; the problem was, at least in its origin, a monetary one, and no institution could have presented better guarantees from the viewpoint of the general interest.

But the extension of the rôle to the commercial domain brought it about that the proper competence of the central bank was soon overstepped: whatever may have been the capacity and the devotion of the directors, the problems presented were of such scope, both in the realm of theory and in that of practice, that hasty and insufficient solutions had necessarily to be improvised.

From the viewpoint of monetary stability, the end was no doubt attained, or nearly so, in many cases. A whole series of currencies could thus remain theoretically fixed at their earlier level with respect to gold. But the price that had to be paid to obtain this result often exceeded all that had been feared, and maybe also in some cases what it was worth.

Section III. Moratoriums and standstill agreements.

Measures of the sort that we have just been considering were for the purpose of dealing with immediate difficulties —with situations which arose day by day. But it was also, and more particularly, necessary to liquidate the past, or at least to prevent it temporarily from weighing too heavily upon the present. This required that the service of the foreign debt should be lightened; but the problem presented itself in very different guises—long-term debts and short-term debts, public debts and private debts, interest payments and amortizations.

The case of Germany is typical; let us take it as the basis of our study on this point.

On Monday, July 13, 1931, there came the astounding news that one of the four great German banks—the famous D Banks—was not opening its doors. Promptly thereupon an extended moratorium was proclaimed in Germany for all payments, both domestic and foreign. The Government of the Reich had recourse to the exceptional method of *Notverordnungen.* Assisted by the *Reichsbank,* it took in hand the actual control of the economic and financial situation.

Within the country, it was led to participate most closely in the reorganization of the great banks, particularly through the bringing in of considerable fresh capital. The German people submitted with admirable discipline to restrictions and constraints that might well have been thought impossible in the economic field. Little by little, the domestic situation grew better, the restraint was relaxed, and a normal financial movement was reestablished.

But as regards foreign creditors, the moratorium measures remained in force. All the funds loaned in Germany were blocked. All the sums due abroad by Germans were made unavailable. There was naturally a very strong reaction. The German default embarrassed the great markets, and plunged innumerable banking and commercial houses abroad into inextricable difficulties.

A conference was convened, to bring the Germans and their foreign creditors together. It met at Basle in August, 1931. Besides Germany, eleven countries were represented in it. The discussions opened in a painful atmosphere. The creditors talked of law, justice, and the sanctity of obligations. The Germans talked of facts, impossibilities, and practical conditions. Harsh words were used—understandable but useless. An agreement nevertheless had to be reached: none could escape it. The creditors had to choose between either an official moratorium, through an act of authority, without any attenuation, and with the general disadvantages of a unilateral and flagrant violation of contracts; or a recognition of the inevitable, with guarantees and compromises. They were wise enough to decide upon the second alternative.

Here are some of the main lines upon which the agreement rested. It extends to capital loaned for short or medium terms to commerce, banking and industry. All the funds are retained where they are. The credits granted from abroad, and especially those that are realized in the form of drafts or acceptances, remain in force. In return, guarantees are given both for the exchange, and for the good ends of these operations. Claims in marks may be virtually transferred into the currency of the creditor, at his option. Bad debtors, up to a certain proportion, may be changed; and their position will be taken in charge, but for a five-year consolidation, by the *Golddiskontbank*. The interest due will be paid. Certain repayments of capital, in the form of monthly instalments, will be made abroad, provided that the *Reichsbank* may be in a material position to do so. All the foreign creditors, whether or not they participate in the agreement, will be put upon the same footing; no discrimination will be made at any time.

This first agreement was made for six months. It goes without saying that it had to be renewed; the causes that had made it necessary were far too deep for any hope of having them disappear within a few months. Twice it was taken up and prolonged for twelve months.

Although modified in its details, adapted to the necessities of the case, and made more flexible, it nevertheless remained upon the original basis.

The agreements reached with the other countries, Austria and Hungary in particular, present the same general features.

*   *   *   *   *   *

Let us now see, then, what are the disadvantages and the deficiences of these standstill agreements.

1) To begin with, they are only a palliative and by no means a remedy for the trouble. They continue to treat as mobile short-term funds which are, at least in part, and perhaps in greater part, immobilized and transformed into long-term. Doubtless the creditors are most of them not in a position to do away with the short-term character of their advances. They themselves have received these funds and are responsible for them in that form; they must, under the penalty of ruining their own position, keep them short-term. There should therefore be an intermediary placed between them and their debtors, to take their place, to make their advances liquid for them, and change to long term the obligations for the debtors.

2) In stabilizing the relations of credit at a given moment, these agreements have prevented a normal process of cure and of adaptation.

They have, in effect, suspended not only the transfer of funds abroad, but also, in the majority of cases, the movements of these funds within the frontiers. Thus, the sums deposited in a bank cannot be used for payments within the country; if a firm enjoys an acceptance credit, this must be maintained for it. Such provisions as these put the foreign creditor into a position inferior to that of the national creditor. That is a flagrant injustice. A German who has an account in *Reichsmarks* does what he pleases with it; the foreigner, caught by the moratorium, cannot do so. But the insistence of the German leaders upon this point can be understood; if the holdings of foreigners were to be made free within the country, the standstill would promptly be evaded; they would be devoted to payments for the purchase of German merchandise, and thus the past would come again to upset the present equilibrium of the exchanges.

It is nevertheless true that a situation so evidently unjust cannot be prolonged. The insufficiency of the present agreements is clear.

3) The rigidity of the economic organization, resulting from the application of these agreements, has serious consequences, as much for the creditors as for the debtors. The former, apart from the enormous inconvenience due to the prolonged unavailability of their holdings, find themselves not in a position to take the precautions for security which are the rule in business life. Because at a given moment one has thought it possible to enter into relations with a firm or with a bank, it does not follow that one may continue this confidence indefinitely. It often happens that the credit position of important houses changes greatly with the years. This eventuality is still more likely in times of crisis. In short, the abnormal immobility which the standstill agreements impose upon the creditor very often increases his risks, and puts in danger the ultimate recovery of the claim.

Now, this transformation is manifestly the direct result of the unilateral decision taken by the interested state. It is a case of a " *fait du prince* ", for which the foreigner is entitled, in all equity, to demand account and reparation.

To give effect to this just view, it has on various occasions been proposed to have the debtor's state assure the good ends of the operations affected by the moratorium. But objections have arisen, particularly (although it may seem strange at first sight) on the part of the creditors. Some are afraid to see the commercial character of their credit thus modified. To these, satisfaction might have been given by having the state's guarantee apply only as a sort of additional endorsement. Others were doubtful lest such an extension of the state's responsibility should diminish its capacity for payment and the scope of its credit for its other obligations, whether past or future.

As for the debtor state itself, such a crystallization of a whole field of its economy tends further to retard the necessary adaptations to the crisis. A part of the capital lent from abroad is found to be not only immobilized, but actually lost. The conclusion of the agreement, in making it impossible for the creditor to put an end to his relations with his debtor, keeps going businesses of which nothing remains but a façade. The cure which ought to be brought about through the disappearance of the weak and the incapable, and through the redoubling of the efforts of the others, is thus postponed. The first effect of this is a prolongation of the crisis, and actual weakening of the possibilities of ultimate recovery in the protected country.

4) This is not the only way in which the standstill agreements have weighted down the development of the world crisis.

They contemplated and made possible the repayment to the creditors of a certain portion of the capital loaned; and needless to say, this portion was wholly withdrawn as quickly as possible. It is enough that capital should be threatened with constraint, for it to seek at once to free itself by flight.

On the other hand, the advances affected by the moratorium having become what the specialists call a bad risk, it was certain that the interest rates imposed by the creditors would be high; such is the rule of business.

So, the sums to be transferred abroad by the debtor countries remained relatively large, and their transfer was so much the heavier because obviously there was no new arrival of fresh capital. The sole method of transfer consisted in the exportation of a surplus of goods.

In fact, then, the debtor country met its obligations, reduced but still abnormal, by liquidating upon foreign markets a supplementary portion of its stocks of finished products and raw materials. This additional amount, thrown into markets already disorganized and gorged, could only increase the pressure, the disorder, and the fall of prices—in other words aggravate the crisis.

5) It is only fair to recognize that these criticisms are applicable not so much to the standstill agreements themselves as to the underlying conditions which have made necessary their conclusion. It must be emphasized that these agreements were only a momentary compromise, that they have not resolved the fundamental difficulty, and that it is necessary to continue, under their temporary protection, the search for adequate definitive remedies.

It should be added, too, that they were limited in their extent as in their duration. They covered only a part of the short-term indebtedness abroad of the interested countries. The obligations of public organizations, such as cities and provinces, remained outside, and had to find some other solution.

Be that as it may, let us recognize, on consideration, that these agreements—the fruits of an empirical wisdom and of mutual goodwill—have been of use. They have saved face, by avoiding a breach of contract which would otherwise have been inevitable. They have permitted the gain of precious time and the preservation from ruin of working institutions. The debtors have carried them out with a full and persistent loyalty, thus assuaging in part the justifiable bitterness created by the declaration of the moratorium.

The renewals have made it possible to point up the details, and to lighten them to some degree. Moreover, individual efforts, pursued in an atmosphere of mutual understanding, have already made it possible to liquidate a certain number of cases.

Certainly, the definitive solution would be hastened if it were possible to put into the form of long-term investments the funds which have in fact been immobilized, and thus to do away with appearances which no longer correspond with the realities.

Many provisions of the agreements, as renewed, have foreseen and facilitated such transformations into long-term obligations. The debtors themselves are trying to go as far as possible in this direction. The improvement of the internal conditions of the interested countries will open up new perspectives in that direction. It appeared, in January, 1933, that, on the faith of more optimistic information regarding the future of German industry, a number of American, Dutch and Swiss creditors were utilizing their blocked holdings for the purchase of securities—bonds and shares in electrical and chemical enterprises.

Perhaps these agreements will thus evolve little by little towards an automatic liquidation, at least in part; that would either make unnecessary, or would greatly facilitate, the conclusion of a definitive operation, bringing to an end this painful chapter in the history of the crisis.

Section IV. Clearing agreements.

Measures of protection taken unilaterally by some states are likely to lead other states, by a direct reaction, to take similar measures. There were few countries strong enough and sound enough to avoid being caught in the machinery. But even these sometimes found themselves bent into attitudes contrary to their principles and to their wishes.

On the other hand, even the countries which had surrounded themselves with the most impermeable barriers, felt the absolute necessity of maintaining at least a minimum of contacts, and they tried to organize an embryo of international relations.

From this double concern there arose and came into use a method of making payments, known under the name of " clearing agreements ". This refers to international conventions under which two countries undertake to settle their mutual commercial transactions by entries in accounts opened with their respective central banks, these accounts to be liquidated in principle by setting them off against each other.

4

Let us examine their theoretical working. As an example, let us take the agreement made between Belgium and Hungary about the middle of 1932.

Many Belgian exporters, having delivered goods to Hungarian clients, had no means of withdrawing from the country the amount of their claims. Moreover, a number of Belgians had been taken by surprise by the exchange restrictions decreed in Hungary, and their holdings were tied up there. The Belgian Ministry for Foreign Affairs was harassed with protests and complaints from Belgian nationals, calling for the support of their Government in cases in which their rights had been denied and in which they found themselves without means of enforcing them before the courts.

On the other hand, Hungary desired to assure itself of further trade outlets, obtain additional foreign currency, and make more effective its control over exchange transactions.

This latter point was particularly instructive. The fact was that, in spite of all the efforts of the political and financial authorities, there had been created a sort of bootleg market, where the Hungarian currency, the *pengo,* was traded at a depreciated rate. The Hungarian importers, in order to pay for their purchases, went to the central bank to exchange *pengos* against foreign currency at par; whereas the foreigner who had to meet the price of Hungarian merchandise succeeded in finding *pengos* at a reduced rate in the " black exchange ".

The two parties, Belgium and Hungary, tried by the convention to kill two or even three birds with one stone.

For the purposes of the agreement, the exchange of the *belga* for the *pengo,* and *vice versa,* is made at monetary parity. The Belgian importers of Hungarian goods are required to pay the agreed price to an account opened in the name of the National Bank of Hungary in the books of the National Bank of Belgium; and this account is kept in *belgas.* Meanwhile, the Hungarian importers must pay the value of the Belgian merchandise which they take to an account opened in the name of the National Bank of Belgium in the National Bank of Hungary. Notifications of these payments are made on either hand. They definitely discharge the paying party with respect to his foreign creditor. In short, the exports from Hungary into Belgium are represented by an accumulation of *belgas* to the credit of the National Bank of Hungary, and the exports from Belgium into Hungary by a sum in *pengos* to the credit of the National Bank of Belgium. If the value of exports is equal for both, the two banks are reciprocally creditors and debtors towards each other to amounts which, converted on the basis of monetary parity, are equivalent; and the banks have only to close their entries in order to settle the whole thing. What could be more simple?

Unfortunately it does not go at all that way in practice.

Belgium desired to get back the sums blocked in Hungary by the declaration of the moratorium. Hungary wanted to find available, after payment for her imports, an asset in *belgas*—that is to say, in foreign currency—for the purpose of assuring in part her financial service abroad.

So it was decided that the sum in *belgas* produced by Hungarian exports into Belgium should be divided into three parts—one, of 45%, should be proportionately divided among the Belgian nationals possessing commercial claims blocked in Hungary; a second, of 35%, should be placed at the free disposal of the National Bank of Hungary by the Belgian Clearing Office; and finally, a third, of some 20%, should serve to pay Belgian exporters the price of their deliveries in Hungary. On paper, this division appears satisfactory enough. Yet, as was noted immediately, in order that the agreement should function regularly, Hungarian sales to Belgium had to be very much larger than Belgian sales to Hungary. The proportion must be four to one in favor of Hungary, if the Belgian producers were to be paid without delay. That was indeed the intention of the Hungarian signers of the agreement; Article 10 says clearly that Belgium

will use every effort to increase its purchases in Hungary with a view to hastening the amortization of the old credits against Hungary and with a view likewise to paying for new sales in Hungary so far as possible by a set-off.

But could it be expected that these hopes would be realized? Would the conclusion of this agreement favor the purpose in view? Not at all.

The Belgian exporters, far from finding in the establishment of this system a reason for diminishing their activity in Hungary, saw therein, on the contrary, a reason for developing it. Until then, many had considered Hungary as a closed market, since they could find no means of being paid from it. But the day when the establishment of a system of compensation was announced, they believed themselves sure of payment in *belgas*; amid the universal disorganization of foreign markets, Hungary seemed to them like solid ground. It was an illusion, but many held it for some time.

Furthermore, apart from the conclusion of this particular agreement with Belgium, the whole system of the moratorium and exchange control applied by Hungary had had the effect, within her frontiers, of hindering an adjustment of prices and of the conditions of production to the continual fall of world prices; deflation, indispensable as soon as the currency was being maintained at its former level with respect to gold, had been artificially stopped. Prices were therefore comparatively higher in Hungary than in Belgium. Once they were assured of receiving in *belgas* at parity the value of the *pengos* paid, the Belgian producers found in Hungary profitable conditions which necessarily favored their exports.

Inversely, the existence of a bootleg market, where Belgian importers could find *pengos* below par, tended to diminish not the actual Hungarian exportations but the payments for them through deposits in *belgas* to the credit of Hungary's account with the National Bank of Belgium. It is true that the convention made this latter mode of payment obligatory for every Belgian, as well as for every Hungarian. But when the interest in fraud is considerable, fraud becomes irrepressible.

Thus the establishment of the new system did not at all modify, but in certain cases even favored, the strength of tendencies which worked against the end in view, and made impossible its regular functioning.

Experience furthermore revealed a long series of additional disadvantages.

Hungary absolutely needs certain products that she can only find abroad. For these products she had, in her own interest, paid in foreign currency, regardless of her own restrictions. Certain Belgian firms, had continued to deliver thus to Hungary merchandise for which they had been paid to the last cent and without delay in foreign currency. Then came the agreement. These were important and strong firms who were not willing either to evade the law or to suffer the inconveniences of it. They suspended their shipments to Hungary. Foreign competitors, who remained free, at once took their places. We have thus lost a fairly remunerative possibility for our exports. What replaced it? Perhaps the exportation of other products; but they will only be paid for in the manner contemplated by the agreement—that is to say that settlement for them is put off to some future date, probably far away. Is that the result that was wanted?

The payment by entry in an account with the creditor bank definitively discharges the debtor. And at once the actual guarantees, which were attached to the credit, are done away with. The creditor thereupon finds himself in possession no longer of a claim with a fixed term and backed by reliable guarantee, but of a right in a common fund—a right which remains threatened, as in the past, by all eventual " faits du prince "—a right with the maturity date for its satisfaction completely undetermined, and without compensating interest in return for the delay. In effect, the date for the settlement of this claim depends ultimately upon the movement of trade between Belgium and Hungary, its volume, and its direction—elements over which the private business man has obviously little or no control, and whose course nobody can foresee. It is doubtful whether such a change makes it easier for a creditor to discount his claim at the bank.

The results of ten months' experience confirm the conclusions of this analysis. The sums accumulated in pengos to the account of Belgium in the National Bank of Hungary are several times larger (converted at par) than the amount in *belgas* accumulated in Belgium in favor of Hungary. It is clear that none of the purposes in view have been attained. The Belgians who believed that they had found a market opening soon lost their illusions, and many of them regret having taken a road on which they again find themselves bogged. The Hungarians have no greater reason to feel satisfied. The balance between their country and ours has not at all improved.

The partisans of the system reply that, without it, the exporters would have got nothing at all, and that it is better than nothing to receive ten or twenty per cent. at more or less distant intervals.

Is not this a sophism? We have seen that, in certain cases, the system has put an end to sales duly paid for in foreign currency. Moreover, many would have preferred not to do business at all if they had foreseen that they would be paid with such slowness.

However that may be, the negotiations pursued by Belgium with other countries on this subject have not been more encouraging. One of these cases is quite typical.

An agreement of this sort had been signed with Yugoslavia. The day when it was to enter into force, we learned with surprise that exchange operations, made on the free market with a discount of 25% for the *dinar,* had nevertheless been approved, or at least semi-officially tolerated by the authorities. Now, our convention contemplated that the conversions of *dinars* into *belgas* would be made at parity for the purpose of the entries on account. Under these circumstances, to impose upon our nationals the obligation of paying in conformity with the agreement amounted to placing them, as regards their purchases in Yugoslavia, in a position clearly inferior to others. That was impossible. The application of the agreement was therefore suspended.

After these experiences, there was less and less disposition in Belgium to extend the system.

* * * * * *

Yet, despite all the disadvantages that we have pointed out, some clearing agreements put into effect in Europe seem to work to the satisfaction of the parties; France signed several of them at the end of 1932. How can we reconcile these facts with the objections to which we have referred?

Let us first note that, in the example that we have been considering, the two contracting countries find themselves in radically different situations. One has a strong currency, and free exchanges; the other, an artificial and limping monetary situation, and a strictly managed economy.

When, on the other hand, an agreement for set-offs is established between two countries confronting like difficulties, whose currency systems are about at the same level, and whose economic positions are similar, the majority of the criticisms we have made cease to apply. It is only a matter of regulating a little more strictly relations which are already placed upon an altogether artificial footing.

A variety of experiences confirms what has just been said, in both directions. Thus, as between Switzerland (with a strong currency) and Austria, the results have been disappointing. On the other hand, as between Austria and Hungary, the system of set-offs has worked regularly, although on an abnormally low basis. As to the attitude of France, it is explained in part by the economic system that she has adopted. Although her currency is very strong, she has gone far in the direction of an artificially managed economy, having recourse to all the protectionist methods, and in particular to contingents that are numerous, variable, and fixed only for short periods. She can thus more easily correct the disadvantages demonstrated by the agreements as circumstances dictate. We should add, moreover, that her undeniable political influence over certain of the contracting countries gives her sometimes the opportunity to impose on them her viewpoint, but sometimes also the willingness to take upon herself grave disadvantages for the sake of other objects of national interest.

England and Holland have refused to take this course. This attitude will surprise nobody, on the part of countries which understand the fundamental rules of international commerce by virtue of having practiced them upon a vast scale. Indeed, let us enlarge the angle at which we have thus far considered these set-off agreements. We see that they rest upon a certain presumption of principle. They take it for granted that the commercial relations between one country and another ought to balance—failing which, they could not be set off against each other. Now, nothing could be more mistaken. The economic equilibrium of a country, with respect to the rest of the world, is not arrived at by adding up the particular equilibriums reached with each of the other countries; it results from a totality of relations, some representing a debit, others a credit balance—relations which are equivalent only as a whole, and on final balance. To arrive at this final and fruitful equipoise, it is indispensable that the commercial balance of one nation with certain others should lean heavily to one side or to the other; and that counter-weights thus be established where they are necessary.

The maintenance of such a general equilibrium demands a great flexibility in particular relations; a credit balance of today must become a debit balance tomorrow, else the general equilibrium would be impaired.

But, contrary to these rules which are fundamental and of current application, the set-off agreements on the one hand claim to establish an equilibrium of commercial balances upon a bilateral plan, and on the other hand, tend to cast commercial relations in a rigid, fixed and artificial mold.

These objections nobody can deny. Even the most positive partisans of the agreements acknowledge them at least in theory. They are the first to declare that these arrangements can have only a temporary value, that they represent an emergency device, and that they will disappear with the crisis: and that is why they have been for short terms, often of three months, renewable, but denouncable with a very short period of notice.

Be that as it may, any policy which misconceives principles is dangerous. It quickly leads into blind alleys, from which escape must sometimes be dearly paid for.

* * * * * *

In the confusion of ideas, many propositions have been

put forward, all of them seeking by means of set-offs to find a solution for the difficulties in the exchange of goods. It is for this reason that there have been taken up insistently, in various quarters, plans for the set-off of goods, that is, in fact, the direct exchange of products—the old fashioned barter. I have known to be developed with conviction, and studied with attention, complicated projects for the organization of international barter, under such sonorous names as " bank for international compensation in merchandise ".

A trace of these ideas is also to be found in several of the clearing-house agreements. It is provided that, under special authorization, transactions based upon the direct exchange of products will be exempted from the obligation to pass through the accounts opened at the central banks. It is to be noted that there is in this a serious inconsistency with the theory of currency set-offs, as we have explained it; the merchants who follow the regular routine are thus deprived of a portion of the eventual advantages of the set-off arrangements, and bear an additional share of the general charges under the agreement. But in the artificial realm of these semi-directed economies, one contradiction the more is no great matter; and this one has in fact often been found to justify itself.

But are we not confronted here with a confused idea?

At the end of all commercial and banking operations, there is an exchange of goods. Commercial relations bring buyers and sellers together " in space "; the operations of credit bring them together " in time ". Obstacles that have been placed by public interventions in the way of the circulation of goods, have in many cases prevented commerce and credit from having their useful effects. Normally, it is by means of a complex organization, admirable in its suppleness and solidity, the result of long experience, stretching throughout the whole world—in a word, through the activity of commercial and banking firms—that the sought-for vast set-off of goods is effected. To replace all this organization by a single institution, centralized, heavy and rigid, is a manifest impossibility.

But even if it could be done, the actual difficulty would remain undiminished. Why would it be easier to induce any country to abandon its protectionist attitude after the creation of such a set-off institution, than before? In short, such projects lose sight of the fact that the interchange of merchandise takes place normally through the habitual channels of commerce, and that it is the obstacles placed in the way of the traditional methods of distribution of goods which lie at the root of our troubles. Suppress these obstacles, and it will soon be seen that there is no need to fear any failure of private initiative; it will fulfill all the necessary intermediary functions for the interchange of goods throughout the world, and for their universal set-off.

CHAPTER III

THE CRISIS OF THE INTERNATIONAL ORGANIZATIONS

Such a haphazard struggle has led the world in general, and Europe in particular, from defeat to defeat, to the verge of utter rout. One may ask what, amid this chaos, has been the rôle of the international organs such as the League of Nations and the Bank for International Settlements, and why it is that their action has not made itself felt more effectively. The reason is that those institutions themselves lie under the weight of events, and are passing through a crisis of their own which paralyzes them or at least restrains them in their efforts.

Section I. The League of Nations.

The League of Nations is of course, by its very nature, the first to feel the effects of the ultra-nationalistic tendencies in the world. Deprived of all means of sanction at the time of its establishment, it can act only by way of persuasion. Its authority is purely moral; it can bring about action only if it is supported by the goodwill of the leaders of the nations, and assured of the earnest support of a vast portion of public opinion. But at the present time, these two bases are lacking.

From its beginnings, the League of Nations has had its detractors and its partisans. The former have taken towards it a purely negative attitude, made up of skepticism, irony, and pseudo-realism. Among the latter, there are many who believed that in it they had seen Minerva spring full-armed from the head of Jove, and have forthwith expected miracles of it. Disappointed in their hopes, awakened from a beautiful dream to a prosaic reality, they are nowadays burning the idol that they worshipped. It is among them that the weak point in the psychological position of the League of Nations is to be found at the present time.

But it is a profound error to try to skip steps in matters of

45

international politics. Time is an indispensable factor for the construction of any work which is to endure.

Our times present, more than most others, the spectacle of opposing forces—some centripetal, the others centrifugal. The principle of nationality, after having favored the reconstitution of some great states, broke up others, and resulted in the formation of a series of small states which were all the more wildly nationalistic because they represented a violent reaction against a former state of things. Yet the progress of technique, and the extension of markets—in short, the latest phase of economic development—made the political separations more artificial and more troublesome, and should have led to larger understandings in the material field.

The Treaty of Versailles was but one stage in this struggle between contradictory tendencies; and it bears that mark upon it. While dividing, on the one hand, it nevertheless sought to bring together, on the other, by creating the League of Nations.

Even if it had been born under the best auspices, the League of Nations could have grown only slowly. We have been spoiled by the acceleration of the rhythm in the economic field. In politics, this rhythm changes slowly if at all.

But the League of Nations was mutilated at its birth by the abstention of the United States of America. The Americans have played an exceptional rôle, since the war, in the political life of the world. That is explained in part by their decisive intervention at a critical hour of the war, by the victory, by their claims against Europe; but also, and especially, because their enormous power is relatively recent, and brings a new element into the whole diplomatic set-up.

So, when the attempt was made to anticipate events by placing under the aegis of the League of Nations problems not yet ripe for solution, there came and had to come either definite defeats or at any rate impasses.

But this general explanation is not sufficient. The direct responsibility of governments must also be taken into account.

On many occasions, and in essential questions, it has happened that the decisions taken at Geneva under the influence and in the spirit of the League of Nations have remained dead letters through the will of those in authority. Witness the famous International Economic Conference of 1927: there was unanimity at Geneva in affirming common rules of action based upon the return to greater liberty; there was almost unanimity among the governments, once the conference was over, in acting contrary to its recommendations. Yet if these rules of good sense had been applied, it is certain that the world would not be in so much misery today.

At times, also, have not the representatives of certain governments, speaking the language of moderation and wisdom at Geneva, been in fact disavowed by those in whose name they were supposed to speak? To declare a policy at Geneva, and to apply a different one at home, is surely not the way to strengthen the League of Nations.

In spite of all the obstacles, the League of Nations has accomplished great things within a secondary but nevertheless important field. With regard to international health, the protection of minorities, and simplification in certain well defined fields of international economy, its participation has been fruitful and indispensable.

Under its aegis have been brought to achievement things that had waited in vain for years. To cite but one example: in 1930-31, a conference bringing together at Geneva 31 states succeeded in bringing about a project of unification in the matter of bills of exchange and cheques—a work that had been attempted at the Hague in 1912, and had been in abeyance since that time.

Lastly, and above all, let us not lose sight of the fact that many of the most important acts which have staked out the international road since the war, from Locarno to Lausanne, have been made possible only by virtue of the personal relationships, the material facilities, and the spiritual influences afforded by Geneva.

When future historians, with the necessary perspective, come to judge of the first ten or fifteen years of the League of Nations, they will be astonished, not as some of us are, that it has not done more, but rather, indeed, that it has so

soon been able to accomplish so many useful and difficult
tasks in so hostile an atmosphere.

*   *   *   *   *   *

But to these general considerations as to the possibilities
and the limitations of action by the League of Nations, must
be added two other more direct comments.

On the one hand, in a universal crisis arising out of a long
series of mistakes and culminating in an explosion of nationalism, it was quite evident that moral influences and general
or remote considerations would be quite brutally thrust into
the background by governments and by public opinion
driven to expedients.

On the other hand, the Geneva institution is for its part
passing through its own crisis, which is indeed influenced by
the general difficulties, but which is nevertheless distinct.

To begin with, there is a crisis in the Secretariat itself.
The officials who compose it, recruited among all nations by
means of a constant and very severe selection, really form as
a whole a remarkable corps. But Geneva is a small town.
The League of Nations occupies too big a place in it. Its
atmosphere is, as it were, saturated. There has developed
there a peculiar *ambiance*, " the Geneva spirit ", which gives
a special tinge to events. That is sometimes a strength and
an advantage, for it is thus easier to achieve the necessary
impartiality. But sometimes, too, it is a weakness. Problems
appear there in a light which no longer corresponds with
that in any of the interested capitals. And the participants
risk being raised above the clouds and thus seeing nothing upon the earth. The danger is the more real because the
contacts between Geneva and the governments are not always
close enough or continuous enough. The officials of the Secretariat thus come to judge sometimes from too great a
height. They have often seen clearly; the directions in which
they have orientated the theoretical researches of the sections
and the technical organizations have almost always been correct and opportune. But they cannot close their eyes to the
contrast between what is recognized as needing to be done,
and what is done; and some of them, conscious of the mis-

takes made in spite of their warnings, and of the opportunities lost in spite of their efforts, allow themselves to be
won over to skepticism, and lose some measure, if not of
their faith, at any rate of their enthusiasm. And this is bad
for everyone.

Moreover the Council itself, and the guidance that it gives,
are by no means free from criticism. The preponderance that
the great powers enjoy in it is well known. But in international affairs, the small countries have often shown more
clear-sightedness, more goodwill, and less egoism and narrowness than the great ones. Their attitude is doubtless explained at least in part by the fact that their own interest was
often more involved, or more clearly discernible in an international course of action. However that may be, many of
the failures can be rightly attributed to the great powers
rather than to the small; and the latter, strengthened by the
facts, demand more insistently their share of influence. In
the interest of all, let us hope that they will succeed.

No impression that the future of the League of Nations is
threatened is to be derived from this explanation. But we
can understand that it has been able neither to end the crisis
nor even to take any strong action with regard to it.

Section II. The Bank for International Settlements.

The Bank for International Settlements was born from the
chance conjuncture of two preoccupations—to give a commercial form to the reparations payments, and to coordinate
the efforts made by the central banks with a view to assuring the normal functioning of the international standard of
values.

The authors of the Young Plan had seen clearly in many
respects. The partial failure of their work has only confirmed the correctness of their fears and of the efforts that
they made to prevent so far as possible the dangers that they
foresaw. They endeavored to remove from the reparations
payments their political character, and to assimilate them to
movements of funds justified by business transactions. Of
course they did not deceive themselves by the appearances

that they created. They had taken note of the fact that, even in an improved form, these payments were possible only if economic life, restored with the clearing of the political horizon and with new and substantial facilities, should get under way sufficiently to carry without strain the reduced burden of the reparations.

There came thus into being at Paris the idea of creating an establishment of a financial character, which should assume a double task—to receive and distribute the reparations payments and then mobilize the equivalents by securities floated on the international markets; and to procure for the business world new facilities in the field of international settlements.

Yet for years there had already been on foot a movement for international *rapprochement* in the monetary field. The troubles which, after the war (and especially during the period 1923-25), had crushed almost all the currencies of the world, had made apparent both the necessity of an international standard of values, and the usefulness, for its functioning, of a collaboration among the central banks.

A man supported by the strongest monetary institution took the lead in this curative movement — Mr. Montagu Norman, Governor of the Bank of England. Only those who saw him at his work from the beginning can realize what he did. The service that he rendered to the economy of the world, during that period, is enormous; and it will remain to his credit, despite the misfortunes of the present time.

He was fortunate in finding, among the principal central banks, able men who gave him their cooperation without reserve. Among them there is one great figure, whom death took away too soon, but whose memory remains fresh— Benjamin Strong, Governor of the Federal Reserve Bank of New York.

Under their inspiration, the cooperation among central banks had become a fact. It had taken certain forms which became standard. On several occasions, consortiums of central banks had been formed to assist certain of them by advances of funds or by the opening of credits. More usually, their headquarters had been at the Bank of England, some-times at the Bank of France. But the need and the desire were felt for organizing this system, giving it a rallying point or rather a seat where regular meetings might take place among the directors of the central banks.

The two lines of preoccupation—those of the authors of the Young Plan, and those of the governors of the central banks—coincided; they were intertwined in the creation of the Bank for International Settlements.

To tell the truth, it was not without some hesitation that some partisans of cooperation among banks of issue were won over to this idea. They feared that the shadow of reparations hovering over the new institution might make more difficult the knitting of relations among the central banks. The opportunity, however, was unique; it was need-ful to seize it, with confidence in the future. And so it was done.

The task was a great one. It aroused enthusiasm, and true devotion. It answered to profound needs. Yet after three years that the Bank has been in existence, has it accomplished many great things? Why has not it, any more than the League of Nations, succeeded in influencing the course of the crisis?

Nearly all the considerations that we have noted in exam-ining the rôle of the League of Nations may and should be repeated, *mutatis mutandis,* in this connection.

The violent reactions that we have emphasized in the national field could not but have their reaction upon the Bank for International Settlements even more directly than on the League of Nations, since their immediate origin was of an economic character. The general atmosphere therefore weighed even more heavily upon Basle than upon Geneva.

As regards the political difficulties, particularly those relating to those decisions on principle to be taken in the matter of reparations, it would seem that they should not have found an echo in the Bank for International Settle-ments. It is, in fact, independent of all political powers; the members of its council represent no government, and are responsible only to each other and to the shareholders; all

5

of them are thoroughly independent characters, and it would be doing them an injustice to bring their objectivity into question. But there would be a certain *naiveté* in believing that, in questions so important as those with which the Bank for International Settlements is concerned, and when their solution carries with it such direct consequences in the political field, the directors of the Bank for International Settlements could have acted as though they lived in an ivory tower. Subdued, and kept in the background, but powerful even so, political preoccupations therefore do weigh upon the decisions which are taken at Basle. Since they are regularly in opposite directions, they have never resulted in bringing about action in one direction or the other, but generally, in hindering action. The Bank for International Settlements has thus kept to a degree of restraint which may be deemed excessive.

As an intermediary in the reparations payments, the Bank for International Settlements fulfilled perfectly what was expected of it. It even succeeded in seizing the very last chance to mobilize a portion of the Allied credit against Germany, just before the crash in the markets. But since June, 1931, the Hoover moratorium has practically suspended its activity along this line.

Germany had, at the beginning, expected a great deal of assistance from the Bank for International Settlements. She invoked, quite rightly, one of the fundamental ideas of the Young Plan, to wit: " If it is desired that reparations payments be made, additional facilities must be procured for the business world, and particularly ", it added, " for Germany ". Let us recognize the facts: the Bank for International Settlements invested in Germany a considerable portion of the funds placed at its disposal; but beyond that, it was quite unable to conceive and to create those new, helpful and powerful currents that the Young Plan had hoped for.

As regards cooperation among banks of issue, if the creation of the Bank for International Settlements has been altogether helpful to it, still it has been impeded by so many factors that a great part actually remains to be done.

From the beginning, the reaction of the City, in London,

has been not very favorable. Was it felt that this threatened London with competition? Was there discontent because the Bank for International Settlements had not been placed in London?

It is certain that the choice of Basle as the headquarters of the new institution has been unfortunate. The city is relatively too small, too isolated, too much apart from the movement of international affairs. We persist in believing that the proposal to select Brussels was the best, and avoided a number of disadvantages. But if not Brussels, it would have been better to take for its headquarters some great center— Paris, Berlin, or preferably London. Here again, an agreement was reached upon the actual solution, because it gave nobody an advantage.

To keep the bank at Basle is a handicap for it; but once the choice has been made, it is much more difficult to remove it than it would have been to put it in the right place at the beginning.

However that may be, the Bank for International Settlements does not find among all interested parties the unconditional support, and the active and effective assistance, which could have been hoped for. This attitude of reserve has certainly contributed to smothering such initiative as the bank might have been able to take.

When England abandoned the gold standard, the situation became tragic. The Bank for International Settlements saw several of its founders and members of its council abandoning the only ground upon which a basis of action might have been found—a common monetary standard.

It might furthermore have incurred grave dangers, itself, with regard to the investments made with its own holdings or with the funds administered by it; but happily, its exchange losses were almost made up by equivalent gains, and on the whole it came through the shock without material damage. But thereupon all hope of playing a decisive rôle in the monetary field, with a view to the struggle against the crisis, had to be put off into the future.

Even the ordinary resources of the Bank for International

Settlements for its activities, which it had utilized during the earlier years of its functioning, were partially cut off thenceforward.

Its deposits came from two main sources—the reserves of the central banks, and the free funds of the treasuries. But the first of these have been reduced because various of the central banks needed them for the defense of their currency, and because others, disgusted by their experience with a chaotic gold exchange standard, have converted these funds into gold bullion. As for the public treasuries, the wave of deficit which rolled over all of them, one after another, soon led to a disappearance of the sums that stood to their credit, both with the Bank for International Settlements and elsewhere.

Furthermore, in its desire to come to the assistance of countries whose monetary integrity was threatened, the Bank for International Settlements had, since 1931, thought it a duty to make a series of advances to Germany, Hungary, Austria, etc. The event proved that the interventions were premature, and probably inadequate. They had been made in order to strengthen the reserves of the banks of issue, in the belief that temporary assistance would be enough to overcome distrust and reestablish normal conditions. But it appeared later on that we were in reality confronting a movement of quite another character, much deeper, much more vast—a movement which could only be dealt with by means of resources, and by means of acts or sacrifices beyond the possible scope of the Bank for International Settlements. The reserves of the banks of issue can and should play their part as a balance-wheel only when it is a question of regularizing such variations in the balance of payments as are in a way habitual or moderate; in the face of outright or permanent unbalance, they are no longer effective.

The *Reichsbank* in April, 1933, has just remitted to the disposal of the Bank for International Settlements, as also to the Bank of France, the Bank of England, and the Federal Reserve Bank of New York, the $70,000,000 which remained due upon the loan granted in 1931. The circumstances in which this repayment took place show clearly that the aim pursued in 1931 has not been fully achieved.

If we were to stop our consideration of the subject here, we would create, quite wrongly, a pessimistic impression with regard to the action and the future of the Bank for International Settlements. Like the League of Nations, the Bank for International Settlements answered permanent needs. It has rendered very real services, both in the matter of reparations, and in a more general sphere of action. It has increased, on friendly ground, and in a mood of objectivity, the personal contacts among the directors of the banks of issue, thus preparing for and hastening the time of further achievements; it has also, in many domains heretofore unexplored, given precision to ideas, and rejected hazardous theories. If it has not done more, let us remember the difficulties that paralyze it, which we have incompletely sketched. Let us above all remember—and this is the fundamental point—that the Bank for International Settlements, like the League of Nations, has only just been born. Its domain, although more limited, is, even more undefined than that of the League of Nations. Here, too, time is an indispensable factor, and it would serve no good purpose to try to go fast.

Let us recognize that the Bank for International Settlements could not have done any more. In such circumstances, no group of men would have been able, without serious and perhaps indeed irremediable imprudence, to carry its activities further. So let us not be astonished that it too has had simply to bow its head under the hurricane of the crisis, and await a happier day.

CHAPTER IV

TENTATIVE REACTIONS ALONG INTERNATIONAL LINES

In the view of future commentators, the middle of the year 1932 will no doubt appear to be for Europe the middle of one of the most painful stages of its perilous after-war journey. The overwhelming misfortune had rendered inevitable some grave modification, whether voluntary or forced, in the conditions of international economic relations. The incompatibility between the characteristics of the crisis and the methods employed to combat it were more and more evident, and became manifest little by little to minds theretofore prejudiced. Besides, if the ideas of narrow national egoism prevail in the confusion of such periods, as did those whose disastrous effects we have pointed out, it does not mean that they have been universally accepted; it is rather because a crisis of will and of authority has driven the leaders and the peoples along the line of least resistance towards immediate interests and objectives less difficult to achieve. Opposing ideas and forces nevertheless exist; experience and necessity develop them; we are confident that they will in their time prevail. Meanwhile, they have already revealed themselves, sometimes vigorously. Without going further back, we find in 1932 several manifestations, several efforts tending towards the repudiation of the policy of international disruption, and towards the organization of realistic and effective common action against the common difficulty.

We will recall three of them, and make a brief analysis of them—the Lausanne Conference, the Stresa Conference, and the Ouchy Convention.

Section I. The Lausanne Conference.

The calling of the Lausanne Conference was the direct result of two important events—the Hoover moratorium, and the report published by the experts who met at Basle in August, 1931.

This report was a solemn and clear warning to the world. It set forth a series of questions to which it was urgent to find solutions if there were to be any stopping the slide into the abyss; one of the most important was the double question of reparations and interallied debts. The latter had been not indeed resolved, but set in a new perspective, by the initiative of President Hoover. The moratorium had in effect introduced, in the political field no less than in the financial, a profoundly modifying factor. The actual relationship which it established between the interallied debts and reparations was well understood to be limited to its duration, that is, one year. But the mere fact of it had altered the whole situation of Europe both in regard to Germany and in regard to the United States. When its term expired, however, reparations payments would have to be resumed on July 1, 1932.

Everyone was aware that it was impossible to go back from this to the Young Plan, pure and simple; too many new facts had intervened; the capacity of all the debtors to pay had been greatly modified under the stress of the crisis; and the moratorium itself, by the mere fact of its coming into effect, had changed the relative positions of the parties.

The invitation to the Lausanne Conference was issued on February 13, 1932, by the six countries most interested in a quick solution — Germany, Belgium, France, Great Britain, Italy and Japan. The meeting opened June 16, 1932. The negotiations lasted almost a month, till July 9, 1932, the date of the signature of the Final Act.

Let us at once note the fact that they were conducted in a very fine spirit. All the parties approached them with good will; but the heaviest sacrifices were of course incumbent upon the largest creditors, such as France and Belgium. If the conference was able to achieve results, that was in great part due to the lofty character of their views.

The perspective in which the delegates at Lausanne envisaged the problem was correct; it is to be found set forth in felicitous terms in one of the first passages of the first provisional agreement drawn up on June 16, 1932, among the principal inviting powers:

Firmly convinced that these problems call for a final and precise solution tending towards the improvement of conditions in Europe, and that this solution should be sought without delay and without interruption in order to be realized *within the framework of a universal settlement.* . . .

At Lausanne, only one question was solved—that of reparations. But general indications were given for the solution of other international problems, and guide-posts were set out to facilitate their execution.

As regards reparations, the solution adopted is radical; it amounts, in fact, to their suppression. The agreed sum upon which they are brought to an end is so minimal, it is hedged about with so many restrictions, and its eventual utilization is to be made in favor of such general interests, that the sacrifice made by the creditors (and more particularly by Belgium and France) can be considered complete. Their delegates had need of courage and of clear vision, to dare to proceed so far ahead of the public opinions to which they must render their account. If the same virtues had oftener and sooner been manifested, it is quite probable that we should not have been reduced to our present extremity.

Of course this renunciation could only give results proportionate to the sacrifice itself, if it was a part of a general programme whose application would assure an end to the miseries of the world. In the spirit of those who consented to it — not without regret, but without *arrière-pensée* — it should find its reward in a restoration of general prosperity. The common welfare demanded many other measures that would, as they themselves expressed it, have to be taken " within the framework of a universal settlement ".

Among these there was one that presented itself to their eyes from exactly the same angle and in the same light as the reparations: that was the payment of the international debts.

Let us leave aside all moral or sentimental considerations, and take our stand, like the delegates at Lausanne, upon the ground of material realities; let us pursue the same end as they, namely to find a return to international conditions suited to the reestablishment of the economic order; from this viewpoint, and in this mood, it is impossible not to come to the same conclusion in regard to the harmfulness of the interallied debts no less than of reparations.

It was understood at the time that the ratification of the Lausanne agreements was subject to the condition *sine qua non* that the problem of the interallied debts would itself be solved in the same spirit, that is, that the parties would seek to promote, by a general settlement, the parallel interests of the creditors and of the debtors.

This was not at all an attempt at pressure, or a tactical position: it was a necessary consequence inherent in the nature of things, deriving directly from the same reasons that led to the signature of the Final Act of Lausanne. If this condition fails—if its realization is defeated—the very basis on which this agreement rests must crumble. The whole thing would have to be done over again.

Of course if one were to examine the two problems from other points of view (such, for example, as the moral justification for payments, the respect for contracts, the capacity of the debtors, etc.), the conclusions would by no means be the same for reparations and for the interallied debts. But such a method would be neither helpful nor correct, since it does not fit in with the facts involved.

The way followed at Lausanne was indeed the only right one; such is the direction in which, cost what it may, progress must continue to be made. Since there was no other reasonable basis for the settlement of the reparations, it follows that there is likewise no other for the settlement of the interallied debts.

But this double question of the international payments of political character, however important, was only one of the chapters of the general settlement that was rightly considered indispensable. The other points, which all related to the economic and financial fields, presented close and complex connections among each other. To essay a solution with any chance of success, it was necessary to have preparations made by means of preliminary studies entrusted to qualified experts. Furthermore, no decisive solution could be found without the cooperation of the United States, since its abstention struck with paralysis every effort for a world cure. Hence there resulted the two well known decisions—first, to confide the definitive task to a general monetary and economic conference which would meet at some appropriate time upon the call of the League of Nations; second, to entrust the preparations for this work to a commission of specialists which would be divided into two subcommittees, one economic and the other financial, and in which it was expressly understood that the United States should be represented.

Yet among all these various and grave problems, there was one which itself was multiple and complex, but which forced itself to the fore with an especial urgency. It was that of Central and Eastern Europe. It concerned a corner of Europe where the exchange restrictions had taken an acute form, and where the crisis, in view of the exclusively agricultural character of the majority of the interested nations, had attained an extreme degree. It was consequently decided to create a committee which should seek means of improving as soon as possible the situation of that part of Europe, and should be entrusted with the task of submitting suggestions to the Committee for the Study of the European Union. Such was the Stresa Conference.

Viewed thus in its main lines, the work of Lausanne appears to us to be an effort of considerable scope, and of correct balance, but even so, merely a beginning. To abandon the work to its fate would be to condemn it to ruin. Yet it cannot be carried on except with the full cooperation of the United States.

The latter understood at once that in working to build the only dyke that could be set up against the flood of the crisis, it would best serve its own interests as well as the interests of the whole world.

Section II. The Stresa Conference.

The ancient Romans already considered Stresa as a place blessed of the gods, and resorted there eagerly. The late summer there is exquisite. I believe that there is no place in the world that is more smiling, and where life is lived more easily.

It was in this setting, made for the delight of the eyes and the refreshment of the spirit, that the Stresa Conference opened. In harsh contrast to the charm of the background, the atmosphere of the Conference, at its beginning, was extraordinarily cold and sombre. The majority of the delegates, and almost all the journalists, had come there with the preconceived conviction that the Conference was doomed to failure.

And there were good reasons to justify these fears. The problem of Central Europe certainly constitutes a special chapter in the book of the universal crisis. There were many reasons for treating it separately and as a matter of urgency; the difficulties there threatened to take a tragic turn. But the origin of these troubles did not lie in Central or Eastern Europe. They derived, like other difficulties, from general phenomena extending alike over the whole of Europe and the world. In fine, the Central and Eastern European crisis, in spite of its special characteristics, was only one aspect of the world crisis; and it was not possible to remedy it by any local treatment.

This view takes on new force when one considers that the essential cause of the misery in Central and Eastern Europe is to be found in the fall of prices of agricultural products, particularly of grain: and what hope could there be of solving this problem apart from the Americas—especially the United States, Canada and Argentina?

The states represented at the Conference formed two groups —on the one side, that of the creditors, or industralized countries; on the other, that of the petitioners, the agricultural debtor countries. As between them, the divergencies of view were, before the meeting, so great that there seemed scarcely to be any means of bringing them together. The majority of the states of the second group came to Stresa with the desire and the hope of obtaining there important material advantages, whether in the form of new loans, or of reductions of old debts, or of subsidies or tariff preferences.

The others, on the contrary, were determined not to grant additional funds to debtors who were already overburdened, being convinced that this policy could only result in disappointments.

There were unfortunately still other handicaps. England, hurt in her interests and in her hopes by the turn of events in East-Central Europe, held aloof in constant reserve. This attitude was furthermore in accord with one of the tendencies of British policy since the fall of the pound sterling—a withdrawal into herself, developing inter-imperial relations, and disinteresting herself in the affairs of Europe. Such ideas, of course, ought not to be carried to the extreme. The English are too capable diplomats not to keep the doors open behind them. Even at this time, when the state of feeling in England forced them to emphasize an appearance of neutrality or of detachment, they were careful not to let the consequences develop too far. The mere fact of this reserve, however, in contrast to the extremely active part that England had taken, in 1923-26, in the curing of the monetary difficulties of several of the East-Central European countries, rendered the task more difficult.

France was, from the political point of view, particularly interested in a successful issue; but for tactical reasons she did not wish to impose a solution which, coming from her, might have appeared suspicious in the eyes of some. To understand this viewpoint, we must recall the defeat of the Tardieu project for a Danubian Confederation.

As to Germany, her own situation created more analogies with some of the debtors than with the creditors; and it had been difficult for her to make much progress, held back as she was by the serious crisis both of her agriculture and of her industry.

In short, none of the great countries, with the exception of Italy, was able or willing actually to set hands to the control levers. The negotiations also opened in an air of uncertainty; and for the first week they were carried on in the most complete confusion.

Have you not thus far got the impression that the calling

of the Conference under such conditions was a mistake? In any case, I believe that it was premature. Perhaps it might have been better to wait.

But in international politics, the calling of a conference is itself a fact—a new element. Once having met, it has to succeed; it cannot just be dissolved with a view to taking up the work again later at the point where it was left off. A defeat at Stresa would have been lamentable; it would have carried with it the most dangerous repercussions in East-Central Europe, and would have exercised a depressing influence upon the future International Economic Conference and upon the preparatory meetings. At any cost, it was necessary to obviate an impasse, to avoid having a majority and a minority report, to encourage those concerned, without verging upon methods that would have been at odds with reality, and to keep open for the future the line of international cooperation.

That was what was accomplished. After the gropings at the beginning, everyone understood that the Conference had to succeed. In spite of all the handicaps, a great good will and a very real loyalty marked the attitude of the participants without exception. It was once more evident that, however great may be the difficulties of an enterprise, efforts pursued in such a spirit are never altogether useless.

The results can be grouped in two categories—the first, of a general or moral character; the others, of a precise or material character.

The exchanges of views carried out during the course of three weeks in the two commissions (one of them economic and agricultural, and the other financial and monetary) cast new and useful light upon the problems themselves. On both sides, there was a recognition of facts which, however essential, had remained unrealized. Here, briefly, are some of these facts.

The situation of each of the countries differs considerably from that of the others, whether under the heading of budget, of currency, of domestic economic equilibrium, etc. There is therefore no " omnibus " remedy — no panacea which can miraculously heal all of East-Central Europe.

But the crisis has weighed down upon them all; it has engendered difficulties which hurt most of them although in different degrees; and it is thus possible to single out certain general considerations which apply to all or to most of them. With this reservation, it may be said that the greatest problem confronting East-Central Europe is the problem of markets and of prices for agricultural products. At present prices, and with the limitations imposed upon exportation, many of them are not in a position to meet the full service on their obligations abroad.

Under these conditions, any new foreign loan would postpone the difficulty without solving it, and would actually risk an aggravation of it. As in the case of the rest of the world, and even more urgently, it is necessary on the one hand that these countries should be able to obtain a higher price for their products and on the other hand that they should be able to export a growing proportion of them.

But all the measures of egoistic protection taken by all countries, one after the other, have simultaneously diminished the possibilities of exportation and contributed to the lowering of prices. The remedy therefore consists in loosening the vise in which they have fastened themselves in the belief that they were protecting themselves. But there, as elsewhere, scattered action has stretched over all a net from which it is no longer possible to extricate themselves save by action in common. And this action in common, while it appeals for the cooperation of all the states of East-Central Europe, extends beyond them, too, and is connected with the problem of the world crisis. In effect, the states of East-Central Europe must begin by setting in order, by their own efforts, all those elements of their economy which are dependent on their action —budgetary equilibrium, equilibrium of the various divisions of production, equilibrium of domestic and foreign prices. As regards the currency, each will decide whether it intends to keep it at the previous level of the gold standard, or whether it will seek for it a new point of international equilibrium; in the former case, the deflation of domestic prices must be carried out realistically.

As for the balance of payments, it will be necessary to bring it towards an equilibrium by coming to arrangements, so far as possible, as to transfers to be made abroad for the service of the foreign debts. But such arrangements can be made only by agreement with the creditors. When all the elements of sufficient equilibrium, domestic and foreign, have been achieved, the suppression of all the organs of constraint and of control will be possible, and must be assured without delay in accordance with a general programme.

The final report of the Conference thus set forth a series of indications as to the situation of Central and Eastern Europe— general considerations, and more direct advice addressed to all those interested, on either side of the barrier. But it contained, moreover, two precise suggestions—the Fund for Revalorization of Cereals, and the Fund for Monetary Normalization.

The former certainly reflects an excellent intention. It is in the right direction, in that, if it could have the effect of raising appreciably the prices of agricultural products, all the other problems of East-Central Europe would disappear incidentally; in particular, the thorny problem of payment of foreign debts would be three-quarters solved; in fact, with the same quantity of products exported, the debtors would pay increasing proportions of their obligations; if the price increase were substantial, the point at which payments abroad could be fully satisfied would be reached without any increase in the volume of the exports. The whole question comes down to whether the projected Fund can effectively accomplish this result.

But what does it consist of? Of an undertaking by the so-called creditor or industrial countries to pay into a common account a sum of 75,000,000 francs every year, for three years. This sum would be distributed among the countries of Central and Eastern Europe in proportion to their exportations of grain.

In fine, the project is limited to promising a subsidy to the exporters of grain.

Manifestly, the sum is trivial in comparison with the factors that have led to the unbalance. How could this trifling assistance modify the fundamental situation of those in interest? That is not apparent. The sums thus received would enable them to pay an additional fraction of their foreign debts; but they would not do away with the necessity of having recourse, in the case of several of the countries, to compounding the debts by agreements with the creditors.

In short, to arrive at a result so unimportant that it does not seem to serve any useful purpose, countries that are themselves at grips with the difficulties of the crisis, and especially with budgetary difficulties, are asked to consent to a financial sacrifice; and for this sacrifice there does not appear to be any compensation, either direct, in the form of tangible advantages, or indirect, in the form of a real healing of one part of the world.

There is a further objection to be made. The countries which are asked to throw good money after bad are not all, or in equal degree, creditors of the beneficiaries. The sums thus paid by virtue of the Fund would therefore go sometimes to creditors who have nothing to do with either the lender or the borrower. In such cases, the Fund would merely cause to be paid by certain countries, which are not interested, claims upon East-Central Europe belonging to nationals of other states. Under these circumstances need one expect great zeal on the part of the eventual contributors?

The proposition made is of course not so simple as the bare outline that we have just presented. Thus, it is stipulated that the participants may discharge their contribution by consenting to tariff advantages corresponding to the sum that would be claimed of them. But whether under one form or another, the sacrifice must be agreed to; the comments that we have made on principle still remain pertinent.

Moreover, the very idea at the basis of the system is erroneous. It is not by occasional subsidies—by temporary and artificial acts of support—that such and such an industry, or Central and Eastern Europe, or the world as a whole, can be saved. These methods have often been applied; if the experience in some cases can serve in others, they would long ago have been discarded. This Fund persists in the rigid and

6

injurious system of *étatiste* interventions and manipulations whose results we have been emphasizing. Even at Stresa, several delegates made express reservations to the idea of the Fund for Revalorization of Cereals. In particular, those representing countries which, like Belgium, had not imposed duties upon the importation of grain, and who would have been the only ones who had to make their contribution to the Fund in money, would have been penalized because of their not having taken measures detrimental to the grain-exporting countries! Briefly, from the time it was first conceived, the chances of the Fund for seeing the light of day were negligible.

The case of the Fund for Monetary Normalization was altogether different.

When the countries of East-Central Europe have (each as regards itself, and in its full sovereignty) completed the setting in order of their domestic position; when the agreements with foreign creditors have settled the problem of the long and short-term debts; when, finally, united action has rid Central and Eastern Europe and the whole world of the multiple coats of mail that are stifling them—then it will be possible to reestablish the shattered currencies of East-Central Europe upon a definitive basis of liberty and stability. But even then it may be that those interested may have need of temporary assistance from abroad in their efforts. Certain of them may be able to do without it; others, not. In any case, such cooperation from outside would hasten the time, and would facilitate for a number of countries the effort necessary for them to take the final step with a view to monetary stability.

In the stabilization operations that brought to an end the period of monetary disorder in 1923-26, this outside assistance was on several occasions assured by the cooperation of the central banks among themselves. That is often the best method; it will find its opportunity again. But at the present time, the arbitrary interventions of states have upset economic and financial relations; they have introduced into them a new risk, of a political character, against which it is impossible to guard otherwise than by political action. Until the reestablishment of a normal situation, it is therefore necessary to appeal to the states to cover those risks which are incidental to their own activity.

Thus took form the idea of constituting, through the intervention of the states, a Fund which should serve eventually to complete the other means of action, and to lend assistance to such countries as, at a proper moment, should desire to fix their currency upon a healthy basis. The operations would be conducted through the intermediation of the banks of issue and of the Bank for International Settlements, but the eventual risks would remain a charge upon the states.

These risks, moreover, if the Fund is managed in conformity with the principles set forth, and if it does not intervene prematurely, are rather theoretical than real. In many cases, the assistance of the Fund can take the form of a simple opening of credits, without actual deposit of funds; it is even possible that that may become the rule; if this were the case, the contribution to the Fund might amount to a simple guarantee of the state.

In contradistinction to the Fund for Revalorization of Cereals, which is a mere matter of subsidy, the Fund for Monetary Normalization does not constitute an act of charity. The sums paid into it would ultimately be repaid to the participants. The gesture thus made would find an indirect but considerable compensation in the general process of healing to which the action of the fund would contribute; it is in the form of a resumption of international business that the contributors would receive their recompense for their act of mutual international assistance.

Reciprocal interests, and the hope of real advantages, surely form solid bases for action.

The name " Fund for Monetary Normalization " itself implies a programme. The barbarism " normalization " was intentionally devised in order to avoid confusion. What is in view is the stability of currencies with respect to an international standard. The word " stabilization " might have given rise in some minds to the impression that it was desired to " stabilize" the currencies at the level at which they had previously been related to the gold standard. As for this, as we have seen, the Conference was careful to maintain an absolute neutrality; each of the interested countries should decide for itself what suited it—whether to maintain the old gold parity, or choose a new one at some suitable time. What is needed is to regularize as soon as possible all the factors entering into or dependent upon currency—that is, to reestablish *normal* monetary conditions; hence the expression " monetary normalization".

Such, then, is the balance-sheet of the Stresa Conference. Perhaps it seems to you to be slight? A description of the difficulties, wise but theoretical advice, two precise projects, of which one appears to be still-born, and the other destined to serve as the frieze of an edifice whose foundations have not yet risen as high as ground level—is that all?

Yes, that is all. It is little enough; yet it is something.

Explanations and advice have by no means been so barren of practical results as one might believe. The degree and the consequences of the crisis in which Central and Eastern Europe were struggling had not been realized by many, even among those best informed, and even among those interested, either at home or abroad. Recognitions of principle, such as those affirming the rights of creditors, in conjunction with examples of good will and of energy manifested by the debtors even if checked by uncontrollable forces, have not failed to exert an influence and to facilitate the necessary concessions. Certain of the debtors understood this in time.

There would be no use in exaggerating the material importance of the two Funds proposed at Stresa. But it would be falling into an equal error to minimize them, or reduce them to nothing. Particularly as regards the Fund for Monetary Normalization, it is probable that under one form or another it will lead to some concrete realization, whose usefulness will prove itself.

But it is not in them that we must seek the real reasons for the interest that the outcome of that Conference evoked, or why it can be said that it was a success.

The thing that was needed above all else was to avoid a shock, and to prevent the two groups of countries, with interests and views so divergent, from antagonizing each other and separating into opposing camps. Such an event would have given a grave wound to the policy of international cooperation, and would have diminished considerably the chances of success of the coming International Economic Conference. It was therefore important above all else to assure a community of views which should keep all roads open for the future. That—the essential thing—was accomplished: a joint report, dealing frankly with the fundamentals of the case, was unanimously signed.

Furthermore, the preoccupations that the discussions revealed, and the state of mind in which they were carried on and brought to a conclusion, form in themselves a result and a favorable indication. Doubtless there were frequent wanderings, and pulling in different directions; that is inevitable and I should even say desirable. Some representatives had taken an unbending attitude because they had come with anxieties and with purposes altogether proper but sometimes covering particular intentions of their own.

But above all there was the feeling that men of good will were loyally seeking means to escape from an impasse where all alike felt themselves to be lost. Several times, delegates were found to change their point of view outright, in the light of new factors brought into view by the work of the Conference. The delegates of rich and powerful countries were found declaring themselves ready to make an effort that was disinterested (not in the sense of performing an act of charity, but in the sense that their effort would serve to promote the interests of other countries) save as their countries would ultimately find their reward in it through a general improvement.

In many places, the final report emphasizes that the problem of Central and Eastern Europe can be solved only in the framework of a universal solution of the crisis as a whole; the suggestions that it contains should some of them be enlarged and extended to other countries, and others be subordinated to conditions that only the future International Economic Conference can bring about. All in all, there was drawn up at Stresa a useful and perhaps even indispensable preface to the International Economic Conference; it is fortunate that it could be written in an appropriate style and mood.

I find a fitting summing up of it in the ideas that were expressed to me at Stresa by a distinguished Polish diplomat: " We are as impatient as children ", he said; " we want to build in a few hours an edifice to last for centuries; in spite of a thousand obstacles, Europe is being built up; talks such as those which are going on at Stresa prove that the idea of universal cooperation is making progress; the way is a long one, but the important thing is to follow it, even though the journey may seem interminable to our hopes and to our impatience." He was a wise man; may the future prove him to be right.

Section III. The Ouchy Convention.

Confronted with the repeated failures of the broad efforts to react against protectionism, the small states endeavored on various occasions to find for the problem solutions which were local and fragmentary, but calculated to diminish the evil, and in a form suitable to be enlarged in order eventually to become a general solution.

In 1930, Belgium, Denmark, Norway, the Netherlands, and Sweden, by the Convention of Oslo (December 22, 1930), decided to renounce reciprocally a portion of their freedom in the matter of customs duties. Each of them undertook not to raise any of these duties without previous reference to the other contracting parties; the latter are entitled, if they think themselves injured thereby, to propose modifications such as would protect their interests; and if these proposals remain unheeded, they may denounce the Convention.

The scope of the agreement was limited. No extraordinary consequences may be expected to flow from it. It nevertheless has had some favorable results. On several occasions, the signatories, following the spirit even more than the letter of the Convention, have put themselves in touch with each other, and come to understandings for the friendly adjustment of temporary problems which had arisen, unforeseen, out of the upsetting of international conditions. Thus, Denmark and Belgium mutually assisted each other in regulating the trade in butter, cream, and meats, which had taken on abnormal proportions between them by reason of the closing of other markets.

But let us note in the Oslo agreement one characteristic provision, which contains the germ of useful developments. The Convention is concluded among the signatories, but is not limited to them; it remains open to whatever other party may wish to adhere to it, provided that the co-contractors agree.

To offer the reciprocal advantages of a treaty to any party whatsoever, on the condition of assuming likewise its obligations, is the best proof of the rectitude of the intentions of those who devised it. The general acceptance of such a clause would be a perfect guarantee against maneuvers detrimental to third parties, and a powerful means of counteracting economic compartmenting.

Unfortunately, again, the example and the initiative embodied in the Oslo agreement remain a dead letter.

*   *   *   *   *   *

Meanwhile, the Conference of Lausanne had met. The private conversations among the delegates of the three or four most powerful countries filled days and days. Two outstanding initiatives reminded the delegates what was the real stake at issue, and what was the direction in which they would have to go.

The first came from His Majesty Albert I, King of the Belgians. In a solemn letter addressed to his Prime Minister who was present at Lausanne, the King called attention, in a few phrases of incomparable vigor of thought and clearness of form, to the necessity of breaking away from the economic errors of recent years. Let us quote this much:

It has been definitely proved that no country is in a position, by virtue of its own forces, to divert to its own advantage the course of economic evolution. Only a concerted action by the states as a matter of international solidarity could bring a remedy to the profound ills from which the world is suffering.

The second of the two initiatives was in part an outcome of the first. Three of the small countries—Holland, Luxembourg and Belgium—signed, on July 18, 1932, at Ouchy-près-Lausanne, an agreement which introduces a new note into international treaties.

The parties undertake a triple obligation as regards their tariff policy.

In the first place, they agree in general not to increase the protective character of the existing tariffs, either by augmentation of existing duties, or by the establishment of new duties.

As among themselves, they undertake, to begin with, neither to augment nor to create duties, and further, to reduce them progressively. It is agreed that the duties will be lowered 10% at the moment when the Convention comes into force; and that this reduction will be continued, through four successive stages of 10% each, for four years, to a total of 50%.

Finally, the parties promise each other to apply to their mutual relations, except in clearly limited special cases, no new prohibition, restriction or hindrance, and to abolish as quickly as possible such of them as exist.

As regards the optional clause which had already appeared in the Oslo Convention, it is here found, not merely repeated, but enlarged, and proposed to all without reserve : " Any third state may adhere to the Convention upon a footing of equality with the signatory states." No approval is required in any quarter; a state desiring to adhere has only to give notice of its intention. There is even this further advance : any state which, without adhering to the Convention, actually observes its provisions, is admitted to share in the advantages of the system.

The announcement of the signature of this Convention made a great impression.

For the first time in a long while, there were states taking a constructive attitude with a view to the lowering of tariff barriers. It was no longer a matter of platonic declarations, but outright, precise obligations that the states undertook towards one another; and they formally invited other countries to follow their example.

Thus far, no adherence has been given. The ratifications themselves have not yet been exchanged. Need one be astonished? Not at all.

The agreement itself encounters one great difficulty: how is the most-favored-nation clause going to work in this connection?

If it were necessary to wait, before appiying the provisions of the agreement, until all the treaties concluded by the signatories which contained this clause had been denounced or had expired, it would be postponed to the Greek Kalends.

The simplest and fairest means of solving the difficulty would consist in giving to the most-favored-nation clause an interpretation in conformity with its spirit; it was originally adopted and incorporated as a method of striving against hindrances to commerce, and not as a method of aggravating or of maintaining them.

Of course, should the letter rather than the spirit of the clause be taken to determine its application, it might be argued that it is generally construed as being "unconditional" and that the suggested interpretation contains in fact a condition.

It must be emphasized, however, that the whole issue is dominated by the essential fact that in treaties of the Ouchy type, which are open to all, the possibility of discriminating against certain countries is completely eliminated.

The advantages that one signatory accords to the other form a totality with the advantages which it receives in return; whoever desires to take advantage of the most-favored-nation clause can do so and claim the application of the Ouchy provisions, but as a whole—that is, upon assuming the advantages and the obligations alike.

Were the acceptance of this interpretation refused, there would remain only one hope; that is that no country would wish or would dare, by invoking this clause, to block absolutely an attempt at the enlargement of markets, which cannot in any way be prejudicial.

The idea is still in its first stage. It is nevertheless attracting attention little by little. Several times, an echo of it has been heard in international manifestations.

Mr. Stimson, in one of his declarations in 1932, let it be clearly understood that the United States would not consider group agreements concluded with a view to the lowering of tariff barriers, and open to all, as contrary to the most-favored-nation clause.

In December, 1932, the *avenant* of the Franco-German Commercial Agreement specified that most-favored-nation treatment would not extend to the rights and privileges accorded by one of the contracting parties to third parties by virtue of plurilateral conventions, provided that the latter were of general scope, open to all, and approved by the League of Nations; but the other contracting party retains the right to obtain these advantages equally for itself by accepting the obligations which are the consideration therefor.

By this clause, the signatories of the *avenant* implicitly recognize that our interpretation of the most-favored-nation clause is correct, and that it cannot be equitably invoked to prevent the coming into force of the Ouchy Convention.

Finally, it is to be remembered that the experts at Geneva endorsed these views in their annotated agenda prepared for the coming world Conference.

An analogous stipulation, to the same effect, is found again in other international agreements, such as the German-Bulgarian Treaty of Commerce of June 24, 1932, and the Belgian-Dutch Treaty of Commerce of February 20, 1933.

These difficulties, and this concern for precision, show that the period of groping has not yet been passed. But the efforts made have not been lost; they have left seed behind them, which will surely grow if the International Economic Conference affords them a favorable atmosphere.

PART III
THE FUNDAMENTAL PROBLEMS

From all these efforts and from all these failures, there emerges an irresistible impression of confusion and unbalance. It is clear that this is no matter of an occasional trouble, which will disappear of itself, but of a profound disturbance, revealing an organic malady and a crucial moment in the evolution of humanity.

In this turmoil, an attentative examination nevertheless allows us to discern some major currents, opposed or divergent, whose meeting creates whirlpools. We have indicated some of them—tendencies towards combatting the crisis by an accentuation of nationalism, yet at the same time sincere and sometimes profound reactions along the line of international cooperation; furthermore, numerous interventions of the political authorities in the economic field, and on the other hand, many efforts on the part of private groups or semi-official organizations with a view to escaping from the noose which little by little is strangling the life of business.

There lie the gravest questions, to which answers must be given if we hope that the march of progress will be resumed. Let us then enlarge our inquiry.

International economic cooperation, or autarchy—which is the method to be chosen?

Whether on the national scale, or on the international scale, what of the tendencies towards a directed economy?

And finally: politics or economics—which should prevail?

Such are the questions to which we will seek an answer in an examination of the facts.

CHAPTER V

AUTARCHY, OR INTERNATIONAL ECONOMY?

No one disputes that modern economy is based upon international relations. That is one of the primary truths so evident that we sometimes cease to be conscious of them. Many men of education but of slight familiarity with the study of these problems are surprised when the depth or the extent of this economic internationalism is pointed out to them. In the web of every national economy are to be found elements of primary importance which in one way or another, but always closely, have relations abroad. Among the products that everyone uses in the course of daily life—whether food or clothing or amusement—which are there whose raw materials do not come from the four corners of the earth? Take the list of the industries of a country: how many are there that can concentrate either their purchases or their sales exclusively within the frontiers? We will not needlessly insist upon so obvious a truth. Let us only recall, as an evidence and a manifestation of this international extension of the modern economy, the perfecting of means of transport, and (at least until the crisis) the flux and reflux of capital across the whole world.

Of course the dependence of a national economy with respect to the rest of the world is measured by the degree of its development or of its progress in the methods of modern capitalism; still it may be said that none has remained altogether apart from international economic life. Countries which are still virtually in the stage of a "natural economy" have themselves been drawn into the movement.

The crisis has brought this fact to attention. For if there is one characteristic of it that no one any longer denies, it is that it is general and universal—general because it extends to all fields of economy, and universal because it has respected no barrier and spared no corner of the earth.

In reality, there is no longer any national economy which

81

is completely isolated. One might have thought that certain countries strong in their own advantages, or in a situation radically different from others, would easily have preserved themselves from the contagion. But there are none such.

The United States finds on its own territories the majority of the raw materials. Its natural riches, in proportion to its population, are enormous. It has at its disposal all the capital necessary. Its domestic market, as regards numbers and purchasing capacity, amounts to a whole continent. Its foreign trade represents scarcely a tenth of its total commerce. Could one imagine conditions more favorable for a national withdrawal into shelter from the storm outside? Yet, after having been a short time held off by the efforts to resist it, the crisis has swept the United States and has caused greater ravages there than elsewhere.

France is a rich country, homogeneous, complete, and balanced; its mode of life has remained far below the capacity of the country; with the accumulation of capital over a long time; with the continuance, in the provinces, of a narrow and laborious life of limited needs easily satisfied locally; with the moderateness of its industrial investments during the boom period—all these factors should have preserved it from any grave shock. They were effective only in postponing the crisis; but it spread to France as well as to the rest of the world. French exports are today reduced to two-fifths of what they were three years ago.

Let us again note that, this time, the predominantly agricultural economies have been no less hurt than the others, but rather more. That is an illuminating indication of the increase of interdependence among all the elements of production throughout the world.

Finally, if there be any country whose present structure differs from that of the rest of the globe, that country is Soviet Russia. The relations between the Russian economy and the economy of the world are reduced to a minimum, strictly controlled, and manipulated to the utmost degree. In spite of everything, the world crisis has had a strong reaction upon the development of the five-year plan and upon the material situation of Russia. The fall in gold prices has weighed upon the Russian economy as upon all others.

There is, then, no exception to the rule.

*   *   *   *   *   *

But if that is the case, and if all national economies are strictly dependent upon one another, there can be no doubt that the change to autarchy would imply for any country whatsoever a violent change of system. Is such a transformation possible of accomplishment?

No, not if it is intended that this be done by following the existing political frontiers, country by country; autarchy, as so understood, is fundamentally impossible.

There was a time when the real economic unit did not exceed, or indeed did not cover, the extent of the territory limited by the political frontiers. But that was a stage corresponding to a state of economic civilization and a mode of life so limited in comparison with that with which we are now familiar, that no people would tolerate being taken back to it. Even suppose (and here we are talking of an absurdity) that some absolute power should succeed in imposing upon the citizens of a modern state a life and an economy such as those of the seventeenth or of the eighteenth century, it would still remain an absolute impossibility for populations so numerous as those of Western Europe at the present time, to live upon their narrow territories by the methods of a local economy.

Where small countries are concerned, the question does not even arise. As for the larger countries, they could not escape the necessity of diminishing both their scale of living and their population. Such an eventuality must be plainly discarded.

But the problem is the more complex when it is a matter not of isolated countries but of groups of nations comprising large populations, and with vast territories covering entire quarters of the globe. Imagine the world cut up into four, five or six economic units, such as the British Empire, Europe, the Americas, and Russia, each group including its colonies,

7

possessions, or spheres of influence. Would it be absurd to imagine that each of them, by applying the resources of modern technique to markets so vast and with natural riches so varied and so complete, could refashion an autonomous economy whose material results would be as abundant as those of our modern international economy? No, it would not be absurd; but it would be absurd to accomplish it or even to attempt it.

To begin with, what would " autarchy " signify in such a case? If the political frontiers do not coincide with the boundaries of the economic group, the problems of international organization and cooperation arise within the group itself, just as we find them confronting us today. The difficulty of solving them would perhaps be in some degree diminished, but would not be changed either in substance or in form.

Supposing, however, that these groups have been established, and that they live each upon a basis of complete economic autonomy: what will happen? Little by little, differences will appear in their respective positions; the level of life in one will exceed that of another; economic antagonisms will again arise. Political oppositions will assert themselves. A whole series of problems, that were supposed to have been avoided, will be presented anew, perhaps with greater sharpness. And the conflict will be settled, either by arms (which would be both atrocious and stupid), or by agreements organizing their economic relations: in other words it will all end just where it should have begun.

In fact, the regrouping of states in a few great isolated economic unities would not cut the gordian knot; its accomplishment would present practically as many international difficulties as a universal solution of the present disorder; nor would it, on the other hand, prevent a return, under other conditions, of the economic and political conflicts that it has sought to avoid. So let us spare ourselves a useless, painful and dangerous stage of the long way towards domination over material factors.

*   *   *   *   *   *

Since we have discarded as impossible or as harmful all the methods of autarchy, there remains to us only one way, that of internationalism. But now we must recognize what that is.

It is not at all a matter of foreseeing, or proclaiming, or even wishing for the fusion of all national economies into an enormous alloy. Let us grant not only the legitimacy, but in fact the desirability, that each of them should keep its characteristics, its own organization, and its natural advantages. Nor is it on the other hand a matter of proscribing regional agreements or group conventions extending to countries whose economies present similar characteristics. Such understandings would doubtless be a first step on the way to international organization, and would facilitate eventual agreements of a more general character.

But the condition must be that, singly or in groups, the national economies pursue their development not one against the other (for we have seen how vain that effort has been) but one with another, each in harmony with the others. That surely involves some temporary or limited sacrifices; but these are in any case inevitable, and in this way they will at least find a large and decisive reward in the improvement of general conditions.

If we recognize that international cooperation in economic matters is the only and the necessary attitude to take, let us realistically draw from that the practical conclusions; they are summed up in words which come back to us like a familiar melody—the suppression of hindrances to commerce, guarantees of a permanent international order, agreements for effective *rapprochement*—in short an international organization in whose shelter prosperity can flourish again with the freedom for the movement of capital and of goods.

CHAPTER VI

DIRECTED ECONOMY, INTERVENTIONISM, OR
LAISSEZ-FAIRE?

" Directed economy "—that is one of those rare expressions
which have the exceptional privilege of exciting either spontaneous enthusiasm or downright opposition. For some, these
two words are synonymous with Bolshevik tyranny; for others,
they conjure up some sort of a paradise where, by a miracle
of knowledge and authority, there would only be, to quote
Baudelaire, " ordre et beauté . . ." ! But whenever words
have thus passed into the realm of sentiment, they become
useless in that of reason. So let us try to forget them, and the
responses that they may arouse in our minds. Let us give up
using them, and set out upon a search, however long it may
be, for so much of truth and of error as may lie behind them.

Section I. Economic laws and practical interventions.

1) The world of economic phenomena is governed by
natural laws. Neither as regards their permanence, nor, alas,
as regards their universality, are these laws any less decisive
than those which we recognize in the other domains of science.
No doubt, as we are here dealing with phenomena which
make direct appeal to human activities, the special reactions
of the personality of each individual do create a margin of
variation which must enter into the application of these laws.
But this characteristic they have in common with all those
laws, whether economic, political or social, which have to do
with the life of man as a social being. As seen in bird's eye
view, they are neither less automatic nor less strong, nor less
enduring.

And why, indeed, should it be otherwise?

Human nature is, at bottom, as true to itself, and as un-
changeable, as the order of progression of the stars. The

constant exercise of individual liberty only confirms this fundamental identity.

But like all natural laws, those of economics are many and
complex. It continually happens that one of them ceases to
produce its effects because another of them has come into
play and prevails over it. Moreover, the circumstances in
which they act necessarily modify the results, without giving
reason to conclude that the laws themselves have changed.
For a century past, the economic field has been undergoing
transformation at an accelerating rhythm, absolutely unknown
in history. The economic sciences, however, are still far short
of a full development; and besides, the field is one in which
intentional experimentation is almost impossible. So we must
not be surprised at our present ignorance, nor discouraged in
the face of the tangle that we still have to unravel.

Can economic laws, of themselves, in free and complete
play, assure or maintain or reestablish an economic equilibrium capable of satisfying the increasing needs of humanity? An answer to such a question in the abstract, in the
doubtful state of our present knowledge, would be just a guess.

2) To get back, then, to actual conditions.

Now, what do we find? That at no stage of the development of mankind has the economic order been completely
left to itself. So there has always been a certain "direction"
of economy.

By "direction" (and this definition is fundamental) we
mean in this connection any intervention of the intelligence
and the will of men for the purpose of making a selection
among the laws of economics, eliminating the action of some,
favoring the action of others, and thus guiding economic
forces and directing them towards a particular aim.

Under most régimes, such interventions have originated
with the political authorities. At some periods, they have
been frequent and urgent, to the point of constituting a
veritable economic dictatorship.

Often, too, the reins of intervention have been in the hands
of intermediary organizations, derived from among business
groups; and sometimes these organizations have been sub-

ordinated to the political power, and sometimes they have themselves dominated it.

We have already pointed out how the scope and consequences of economic laws are modified by the changes in surrounding circumstances. It sometimes happens that the extension or broader application of a rule so far changes its effect that it in fact ceases to operate. The narrowing of its field of action, whether absolutely or relatively, often paralyzes it likewise.

Let us take an example. It is a matter of ordinary prudence and current practice with bankers to require from their clients additional covering margins when the securities guaranteeing advances to them go down on the stock exchange. If the client does not comply in time, he is closed out; the securities are sold, and the proceeds are used in payment of the debt. This rule works without difficulty when it concerns occasional cases. But if, instead, it is applied indiscriminately during a period of general crisis, there is a danger of its turning against those whom it should protect; wholesale executions of this sort drive down the prices of securities, thereby impair other guarantees, thereby compel new executions, and so on indefinitely.

Likewise, if a bank of small importance is unfortunate in its business, it fails; its depositors suffer; but the community scarcely feels it, and things go their way. But where it is an institution whose power and whose ramifications extend throughout the greater part of the economic life of a country, the reaction will manifestly be different; the private interests involved in its fate are so numerous that the matter becomes in fact one affecting the general interests; and it is for the sake of the latter that there must promptly be some intervention.

In short, the evolution of economic conditions, by modifying the conditions of application and the consequences of the laws involved, also changes the traditional occasions and the methods of intervention.

But there has been a period—a moment of economic history —in which the natural laws worked without apparent constraint; that was the period of economic liberalism, whose height was about 1860; and it was, moreover, a period of extraordinary prosperity for the whole world.

Let us, to begin with, note the fact that that embryonic form of world economy, developed at that moment under the shadow of liberalism, was not without organization. In fact, it possessed a center of action, and followed rules which were suggested to it by a hegemonic power. London was its center. England was the power exercising the hegemony— England based upon its incontestable triple supremacy in industry, commerce and finance. This is not the place to inquire into the cause of that superiority; but we must recall that the City was directed by a small group of men whose experience, ability, and foresight actually conducted, with much tact, but with sufficient definiteness, not only the economy of England but the main lines of international economy.

Unfortunately, the combination of happy circumstances and technical ability, which had put the reins into the hands of England, gradually decreased.

We come thus to a time shortly before the Great War. The prevailing situation differs as much from the English liberalism of 1860, as 1860 differed from the beginnings of industrialization. We witness an experimental demonstration of the double adage:—the need creates the function, and the function creates the organ. The need of a definite organization for the production and distribution of goods is especially evidenced by the agreements among producers. They ignore national frontiers. They escape, or endeavor to escape, the domination of politics. They are a spontaneous effort of the economic elements to avoid the disadvantages of dispersion and of confusion, and to organize for definite ends.

But in the meanwhile, nationalistic tendencies are manifesting themselves, first in the political field, then in the economic. The states, now, are entering the economic lists, by means of an accentuation of protectionist measures.

This tendency on the part of states to intervene in international economic relations was carried on and largely developed after the war.

The coming of the crisis removed all restraint upon it.

Today, the world is bowed under the burden of an enormous and contradictory system of obstacles to the circulation of goods. In the face of this widespread disaster, there is none to say, "it is not our doing."

3) We can already pass judgment upon the interventions by which it has been attempted to rid ourselves of the crisis. It is an easy task: the results are so cruel that condemnation is a matter of course. But let us stop and inquire into the reasons for their failure.

Let us represent the movement of business by a graphic line. It is an alternating succession of ups and downs. The crisis begins when the line bends into an abrupt decline; but its origin is at a point well back of that. It is during the boom period that excesses are committed which call for an inevitable reaction. To fight effectively against the crisis, in order to avoid or at least to minimize it, there should be an intervention, not at the moment when the line drops, but rather at the moment when there begins to be a rise above a certain level, not far from the normal; after the event, that point is easy to distinguish, but in practical life it is extremely difficult, not to say impossible, to determine that point with accuracy; yet in every boom period there comes a moment when it is simple to observe and to proclaim that the point of equilibrium has been passed, and that it is time to put on the brakes.

Unhappily it is just at this moment that the "climate"—the atmosphere—is most unfavorable for any measure of restraint. The experience of past crises, indeed, was lost sight of in the present one. The boom period hatched only theoreticians of a prosperity without limit and without restraint—of prosperity at any cost and in spite of everything.

But the efforts made to stop a crisis, once it has been launched, usually do more harm than good. By retarding the moment of the inevitable liquidation, they make it more serious and more complicated.

It has been seen only too clearly in the unsuccess of most of the efforts, made by the cartels, for the maintenance of prices; they have broken down, and had to break down, one after the other. Only those have obtained results who have from the beginning jettisoned a large part of their cargo, followed the movements of the market, and observed a policy of sacrifices during the crisis as a sequel to having kept to a moderate attitude during the boom.

The first cause of failure is to be found, then, in the moment chosen and the purpose contemplated by these interventions—i. e., the attempt to check the fall in prices when the curve of the crisis is in full sweep downward.

A second cause is to be found in the spirit and in the methods generally inspiring these interventions, and more particularly those originating with the governmental authorities.

While our whole modern economy of mass production, of standardization, of concentration of capital, rests upon one postulate—namely, that the world constitutes a single great economic market,—the struggle against the crisis has in fact been carried out on a national basis. The interventions that we have dealt with started from the idea that any single country can and should protect itself by autonomous action, without concerning itself with the effect its attitude is in danger of producing upon other national economies. There is a blatant contradiction between means and end: failure was a certainty. We must hasten to add that in many cases these inadequate measures were the practically inevitable re-action to other measures of control or restraint taken by neighbors; but this partial subjective justification does not in any respect change the judgment to be passed, in general, upon the efforts and the mistakes produced by such methods.

These two reasons are amply sufficient in themselves to explain the failure that was suffered. Yet we should further note a characteristic of these interventions which, even apart from other reasons, would in the long run have made them fruitless. That is that, in many cases, they make the state, or organizations directly dependent upon it, play an active and positive rôle in transactions of an economic nature—a rôle for which it is not fitted, and should not be fitted.

We need not bother to make theoretical proofs of this last declaration against *étatisme*. There is, in fact, a pathetic and already conclusive experiment being worked out before our eyes at the present time—the five-year plan of the Soviets. That is not a matter of communism, but rather, indeed, of state capitalism pushed to its furthest extremes.

The five-year plan is not itself either a success or a failure. Its results are far from fulfilling the ambitious hopes of its promoters. It has nevertheless given Russia a great series of instruments of production, to which it would be childish to deny any importance and effectiveness. But that is not the question. What interests us is to know whether the methods of the industrial *étatisme,* on which the five-year plan is based, have brought results superior to those that the application of the methods of traditional capitalism would have given. I believe that the answer to this question is not in doubt: it is clearly unfavorable to *étatisme.*

Among the very grave defects which the operation of the five-year plan has revealed—and still displays every day,— let us recall two that are of fundamental importance.

In the first place, there are the errors, the inconsistencies and the losses due to the distortion suffered by the directing thought when it comes down from the executive plane to that of the means of execution; and in the second place, there are the defects of adaptation, of cohesion, and of harmony which result from the inability of those in power to dominate all aspects of the infinitely complex problem of the industrial production as a whole.

These problems would deserve an attentive examination; but since we cannot pause for that, let us be content with establishing our contention by the results which the Soviets have reached; in other words, let us inquire whether the cost price of goods produced by the Soviet economy is or is not below that of the same products under the capitalistic economy.

To anticipate an objection, let us at once say that this idea of cost price is quite different in one economy and another, but it is possible in theory to establish corresponding elements in one and the other. Researches on this question have been made on both sides of the barrier—on the Soviet side as well as on ours; and the conclusions have been of the same sort. I shall here confine myself to recalling an opinion emanating from the Soviet side; it estimates that, all things being equal, the cost price under the Soviet economy is still (and it is they who say " still ") two and one-half times higher than that under the capitalist economy.

Let us add, moreover, that even if that were not the case—that even if the cost price under the Soviet economy might by some impossibility be brought below that under the capitalist economy,—our conclusion would not be different; the conditions of life that it demands, the stifling atmosphere in which it develops, the sacrifices that it imposes upon the human personality, would still make it an incommensurable price to pay for a slight material advantage.

And so it will be understood that we discard, without further examination, the hypothesis of an economy directed from one end of the scale to the other by the state.

Section II. Economic policy.

We have thus brought our materials to the workshop, and the time to build has come.

1) Now, these elements appear contradictory: to begin with, we perceive economic laws that are automatic, permanent and numerous; yet it has never been possible to leave them completely to themselves; interventions, more or less numerous according to the period, have endeavored to coordinate and to hold them in check; finally, in recent years we encounter a particularly numerous series of interventions of every sort—interventions whose results have as a whole been lamentable.

A like contradiction is to be found between the hopes that arise and the tendencies that are manifested in proportion as the crisis continues.

On the one hand, experts and laymen are in accord in proclaiming the harmfulness of the thousand measures which stifle international economic relations; they demand that these be abolished or alleviated.

On the other hand, there is growing a feeling of need and

a desire to remedy the economic confusion—the chaos of which the crisis is the tangible manifestation; and an unde-fined but persistent hope for more order, more clearness, more harmony in the economic domain, continues to grow.

We could go on multiplying evidence, for it abounds.

In certain countries, the organization of economic activity is methodically carried out. Let us only refer to Germany and Italy. To be sure, it is too soon to estimate objectively the result of these efforts. And we will do no more than instance them as manifestations of a widespread tendency towards the organization of economy. The Italian experiment, in par-ticular, has aroused in the world an intense interest, for the reason that it is related to a system—to a coherent theory— and is being developed according to a plan whose logical outlines are now beginning to be seen.

The very abundance of plans and projects designed to solve the crisis is another evidence of it. No doubt, good in-tentions are not enough, and one cannot but smile to see how many excellent folk fancy that in sudden wisdom they have found the "open sesame" of prosperity. But along with a thousand manifestations of mingled good faith and igno-rance, we find a series of maturely worked out projects bear-ing eminent names such as those of Francqui or Delaisi in Europe, and of Hoover, Baker or Butler in America.

Let us recall here two counsels emanating from sources as different as can be imagined—one, the highest moral author-ity in the world; the other, one of the most important groups of financiers.

Here are some extracts from the Encyclical, *Quadragesimo anno:*—

Just as one cannot take from individuals, and transfer to the com-munity, functions which they are capable of fulfilling on their own initiative and by their own means, so it would be committing an injustice, while at the same time very injuriously troubling the social order, to take from groups of a lower order, to entrust them to a vaster collectivity of a higher rank, those functions which they are themselves in a position to fulfill.

The establishment of a well-ordered economic régime can be ex-pected only from the free play of competition.

. . . It is therefore absolutely necessary to place economic life once more under the law of a just and efficacious directing principle.

. . . We should nevertheless say that there are, to our knowledge, those who fear lest the state substitute itself for private initiative, instead of limiting itself to aid or to necessary and sufficient assistance.

. . . We believe, furthermore, as a necessary consequence, that this objective [the establishment of a better social equilibrium] will the more surely be attained in proportion as professional and social technical skill contribute to it. . . .

Free competition within reasonable and just limits, and, even more, economic power, must be effectively subordinated to public authority as regards everything which is its concern.

And here are some lines taken from the most recent report of the Société Générale de Belgique:

All the conditions favorable to a broad activity were thus found to exist. Those are the conditions which it would be desirable to have reestablished as soon as possible in favor of a broad spirit of cooperation, while of course correcting such unhealthy elements as some of them contained. By this we mean, especially, that the movement of capital should be appropriately supervised and controlled.

It is important, indeed, that such capital as is loaned should be put to uses in accordance with what had been intended for it; it is especially important that it be employed for productive purposes and for reasonable investments.

Contradictory tendencies, we have remarked. Yes, but only in appearance. When movements of opinion reach such a degree of strength and of depth, it is seldom that they do not correspond to genuine needs and contain an element of truth. At bottom, these two tendencies towards greater liberty and towards greater order are in harmony, and from the elements that we have gathered together, we shall attempt to draw a conclusion that clarifies and justifies them both.

2) At the very beginning, let us with the utmost clearness condemn all those ambitious theories which would have the infinitively complicated mechanism of economic relations, from top to bottom, and in its main outlines and in its details, directed by anyone whatsoever.

All those who are familiar with the conduct of business know that there is an *optimum* size that no enterprise and no group should exceed. Once that is passed, those in control feel it at once; the proportional return diminishes; the organization loses its flexibility and its efficiency; in a word, the thing begins to get out of hand. Doubtless this *optimum* size may vary according to the personality of those in control; but it is a point beyond which it is never, in any case, and under whatever direction it may be, possible to pass without injury.

No other argument is needed in order to understand that the economic mechanism as a whole exceeds in its scope the capacity of comprehension and the power of action of any possible superman or of any possible Sanhedrim.

By virtue of the same criterion, we shall discard, from among the definite plans and projects to which we have alluded, all those which by their extent and by their ambition approximate a general system for the organization of economy, whether on the national scale, or on the international.

3) Yet it is not enough to criticize and to fold our arms. The evil is there, before our eyes, and it is of the utmost seriousness.

The disintegration of our whole economic organization is a fact. Even those whose convictions predispose them to maintaining in its entirety a contrary theory, recognize that, under present circumstances, it would be Utopian to attempt a return to a regime of complete *laisser-faire.*

To get out of the bog in which we have foundered, there can be no question that decisive interventions are necessary—though it were only to rid us of the impediments that other excessive or mistaken interventions have left behind them.

4) But this point granted, what is important is to define what should be the characteristics of such interventions, and also by what authorities and in accordance with what methods this policy should be applied.

The first requisite which should characterize any policy of intervention is that it should be moderate, and limited to those cases in which it appears absolutely indispensable; the second is that it should be confined to allowing the action of economic forces to develop as completely and as freely as possible, without undertaking to replace them or to turn them artificially from their course.

Economists are often inclined to have recourse, in explaining their ideas, to comparisons borrowed from medical practice. I do not ordinarily care much for these, because, for one thing, comparing is not reasoning, and because, moreover, they have been generally abused. Yet there is here a striking analogy. Do men intervene in the biological, physical or chemical laws which govern human existence? Yes, and no—no, in the sense that they do not attempt, and manifestly could not attempt, to supplant the action of such laws; yes, in the sense that they can select among them in order to allow those which favor the quickening and the developing of life, at a given moment and in determined circumstances, to prevail over the others.

The same attitude, it seems to me, should govern interventions in the economic field: recognize economic laws, and let them act to the full while choosing among them in order to give priority to those that favor progress towards order.

To make my idea plain, allow me to have recourse to an example taken from experience. The traditional policy of banks of issue tends to regularize the money market by the maintenance of discount rates. That is a matter of intervention—a control imposed upon one part of the economy. But let us note its characteristics. It tends to facilitate the working of economic laws; it is through their operation that it attains its end. The action of men in this case is principally concerned with reenforcing the action of automatic forces. In recent years, there have been banks of issue which departed from this rule and intervened for the purpose of paralyzing and annihilating the effects of certain movements. For example, in the mechanism of the gold standard, an important fact is that the flow of precious metal into a market establishes there an abundance of means of payment and of credit; to let the gold come, and at the same time to endeavor to limit the normal effects of this inflow, is to intervene artificially, against the stream. Experience has shown that this was a mistake. In the report of the Gold Delegation there is rightly an insistence upon the necessity of a change in attitude and a return, especially on this point, to tradition: intervention should facilitate and sustain the normal effect of the spontaneous movements of gold.

In practice, our maxims may then be reduced to this, that there should be intervention only when an abuse or a danger demands it.

Under such conditions, the policy of intervention would seem to be at once the indispensable condition and the best guarantee of the most complete liberty compatible with the demands of reality.

It would be appropriate here to draw the classic distinction between license and liberty. It is clearly in point.

The accentuation of economic nationalism, to which we have referred, surely corresponds to profound tendencies similar to those that have strengthened political nationalism. Yet it must be recognized that many of the measures of protectionism have been taken by way of reaction against methods of international competition which perverted the laws of normal competition—such as dumping, in its thousand forms. There can be no doubt of the fact that the reestablishment of actual liberty in the international exchanges depends in large degree upon the reestablishment of a minimum of commercial morality in business practice. International agreements regulating and supervising this liberty, reestablished on a basis of equality among states, would represent a type of intervention whose development would be welcomed by all the healthy elements of the business world.

Let us here, as a test, apply our thesis to one of the great economic problems of the hour.

The gigantic progress of technique obliges manufacturers to pay for their machinery within a few short years. They sometimes have to replace it before it is paid for, and thus to exaggerate their recourse to credit. Is not that a waste of capital? Would not it be possible, as has been suggested,

8

to regulate the investment of new capital in order to assure a full return from the old? Certainly not.

Does anyone suppose that there could exist a mind so powerful and so beneficent as to contrive the terms of such a regulation? I remain convinced, for my part, that the capacity of yield of capital is, on the whole, the best criterion of the economic usefulness of its investment. Yet there are cases in which manifest errors may be avoided through the co-operation of economic organs that are better advised or better informed. In particular, there comes a moment, in the course of rising prosperity, when the rhythm of investments inevitably exceeds the normal pace, because they are made in consequence of an excess of credit: at that moment, a policy of intervention tending to restrain credits would be the surest and most effective method, even though indirect, to set a limit to the movement—that is, to avoid fresh errors.

5) We thus come to an essential point. By whom should these interventions be effected? In what hands, to use a happy current expression, should the control levers be held?

Let us see what are the available possibilities.

Within the business world itself, groupings have taken shape, which, under a thousand different forms, and under the most diverse names, have endeavored to bring order into the hundred particular domains of economics.

Agreements among producers have their enthusiastic partisans and their convinced opponents. It is clear that they do present disadvantages. Like the tongue of Aesop, they may be the best possible, and the worst. Their very multiplication, however, shows that they answer to a real need. In my opinion, their advantages outweigh their disadvantages. It would be better to try to keep their usefulness while taking precautions against their special dangers. They unquestionably form an element of order and of regularity in a world which has need of such conditions more and more.

But understandings among producers are only one among the many means to meet this need for order. Other formulas have come, or will come, out of the world of business, whether the initiative in them come from private or from public agencies.

There are capable men who expect practical results from an organization of corporative groups. Is the idea yet ripe? I do not know. I have formed no conviction of my own. I am waiting for further indications, which should be made available as a result of experiments now being tried.

The position that we have taken may arouse many objections. We will refer to two of them, since they give the opportunity to make our point of view more definite.

a) To begin with, the unsuccess of cartels and trusts, in their struggle against the crisis, will be brought up against what we have just said.

But if these interventions have failed, and had to fail, it was precisely because they were made at the wrong time, during the great period of fall in the cyclical curve.

Besides, let us be clearly understood: when we admit the possibility and the usefulness of certain limited and restricted interventions, we obviously do not wish to give approval to all interventions, whatever they may be. If there are interventions that are right and appropriate, there are also many that are foolish and untimely.

We have had to point out the error committed in the course of many interventions in the recent past. We will not cease to emphasize the absurdity and inanity of most of the measures taken by states to hinder the movement of goods and of capital beyond their frontiers. We should also allude to those innumerable lucubrations which sprout under the crisis like mushrooms under a summer shower. Not a day goes by but that the chanceries receive dozens of projects, exhaustive and definitive—not a month that a new theory, baptized with some pompous or barbarous name such as that of the latest arrival, " technocracy ", does not fill the columns of the newspapers and magazines.

Many of these projects or panaceas deal with the currency. To how many people has it not appeared that a modification in the unit of measure of value is the key to the enigma!

And that is quite understandable. The clearest manifestation of the crisis is the catastrophic fall of prices. The gold standard has temporarily ceased to play its rôle as an international standard. In practical fact, business men encounter at every step monetary difficulties—exchange risks, competition with countries having depreciated currency, etc. Vast experiments have been made in the effort to cause a quickening of life, by injections of monetary tokens or supplementary credits into the veins of the organism. Their failure up to the present time has not yet opened all eyes.

But this accumulation of errors, either past or contemplated, shows how difficult it is to determine when, where and how it is advisable to intervene, even with quite limited objectives and means. It is precisely this difficulty which makes any policy of intervention so difficult and so dangerous; and that is also the reason why it must be strictly limited, in fact to those cases in which abstention would be a sure evil.

b) The second objection is much graver and more pertinent.

The object of all these interventions is to create, or at any rate to approximate the creation of, a state of order and harmony in economic relations. But the action of economic groups is confined to a narrow portion of the whole; their viewpoint is of necessity individual, and their purpose limited to their own interest. How could a series of actions—particularistic, scattered, perhaps contradictory—be such as to favor a general coordination of production and of consumption.

Let us at once admit that we here touch upon one of the critical points of the problem. The possibilities of abuse are real, although often exaggerated; moreover, even apart from abuse, conflicts of interest may arise; and finally, it is undeniable that the action of groups, without a general view of the whole situation, has in many cases been harmful to general progress.

We must therefore call to the rescue another element—another power—the political authority—the state.

It is the essential function of the state to establish the balance among private interests in order to serve the general welfare. With regard to economic organizations, it should have a double rôle—to prevent abuses, and to assure the coordination of efforts. But the interventions by which it should fulfill this rôle should keep to an entirely negative character; apart from circumstances genuinely exceptional and unforeseeable, the state should confine itself to holding private initiative within legitimate bounds, and preventing encroachments threatening either the rights of other individuals or the public welfare, without itself undertaking positive or direct action.

If we had to define one of the tendencies now being evolved, we would say that the state should withdraw from a whole series of fields which do not concern it, and direct its tutelary action into other channels, where it should develop, with clearer views of modern needs, a stronger authority guided by a clearer responsibility.

However that may be, what the state needs is not so much a policy of economic direction as a policy in economic matters—in other words, an economic policy. But even so, while duly limiting it, we recognize in the end the primacy of politics over economics.

Let us sum up, then.

We set out with an analysis of facts and practical reactions. We have thus been brought to recognize that general plans of directed economy were only an illusion, and to condemn direct or positive interventions, of an *étatiste* sort, in the economic domain. More particularly, we have pointed out the harmfulness of economic nationalism and of the measures that have almost made it a reality. Yet we have also had to acknowledge that interventions emanating from the intelligence and the will of men were necessary—necessary in the first place to get rid of the mistakes piled up by a thousand wrong interventions—necessary, furthermore, to avoid in future the return of the miseries from which we suffer today. Measures must be taken to put an end to the mistakes and to the maneuvers which have quite definitely led to the absurd and paralyzing reactions of out-and-out protectionism; this is the price of economic disarmament.

But we have seen that recourse should be had to these interventions only when abstention would be a sure evil; and in any case, their action should be confined to utilizing and completing the action of natural economic forces. Such a policy, delicate and dangerous, but indispensable, can be confided only to organizations arising out of the economic domain itself; the state should merely aid them, keep them within bounds, and coordinate them, while taking care that they do not go beyond the framework of the general interest. According to a phrase that achieved an hour of celebrity in Belgium, it would be a régime of sustained and supervised liberty.

These ideas, however just they may be, of course remain very general in character; it is impossible to make them more definite, and still remain in close touch with reality and forego anticipations in which imagination would play a larger part than experience.

What seems essential, however, is the attitude of mind that should be taken with regard to the problems of the moment; and that, it seems to me, is pointed out by the rules that we have suggested. When we find before us precise projects (whether the question is of great public works to be carried out, credit institutions to be founded, or understandings to be reached) we will judge them on their own merits, without a priori dogmatism but with the help of the criteria whose correctness we have come to recognize.

CHAPTER VII

PRIMACY OF POLITICS OR OF ECONOMICS?

One of the forms taken by the confusion of ideas is to be found in this question, asked a thousand times since the war: Economics or politics—which should be preponderant in the views of statesmen?

Many are the good minds giving the answer that it should unquestionably be economics. Many others declare with like energy that it should be politics.

The treaties of peace, in 1919, chose in some points solutions which ignored economics. Yet cannot as much be said, or almost so, as regards politics?

However that may be, the anti-economic seeds incautiously scattered at that time have sprouted; favored in their growth by the inevitable consequences of the war and by the mistakes (which were not inevitable) of post-war politics, they have borne the poisonous fruit from which we are all suffering now. Who can be astonished after all that, to find the primacy of economics proclaimed?

But is not that a confusion? It seems to me that the question should not be put in that way.

The art of governing—politics—extends to the general interests of the country, in their totality, whether in the material or in the spiritual field. The Sovereign can no more disinterest himself in the culture and in the intellectual life, than in the prosperity or the misery of the governed. The interactions of the material situation of a country, and its intellectual outlook, are striking. Was it not increasing and prevailing wealth which made possible those exceptional flowerings of art and of intellect, of which the great communes of Flanders, of Lombardy, or of the Hanseatic League have given us such prodigious examples? Economics is an integral part of politics. Yet it would be wrong to maintain

105

that the whole dominates the part; it includes it, lives by it, is influenced by it, and cannot ignore or exclude it without mutilating itself and perishing. In short, if there are sometimes problems whose character is impressed with essentially material conditions, and sometimes others with relationships of a more general or a more sentimental kind, there are none of them outside of " politics " in the higher sense of that word; any solution which sacrifices some aspect of the multiple material or spiritual reality is to that degree " impolitic ".

But the relative importance of economic problems, among the whole set of preoccupations of peoples, varies greatly in the different periods of history. There are moments of pause—halting-places where humanity catches its breadth in its economic ascent; there are then, within the temporarily harmonized national and international systems of things, methods in the production of goods which permit the economic machine to move slowly, without damage, or by itself.

Need it be remarked that such is not the case in the times in which we are living?

We are passing through a transitional phase. The regime of large-scale capitalism, which during the past century has profoundly changed the basic conditions of our economy, has not reached the end of its course, nor the limit of its possibilities. Great changes are going on under our eyes, following a swifter rhythm than ever before.

On the other hand, the laws of this transformation, and the phenomena that mark its stages, are no longer hedged in by the ancient limits which once constituted political or natural frontiers, particularly those which were due to distances. A national formula of life, which would perhaps assure equilibrium to an isolated people, no longer helps in escaping from or in solving the difficult economic problems which a nation has to meet today by reason of the mere fact of occupying a place in the community of nations.

In such a period of transition and of internationalism, it is plain that the problems of economics thrust themselves more and more into the foreground of the preoccupations of those in political power.

And yet, though that be so, and whatever may be the importance of material interests, we must not fall into the contrary error of believing that they cannot be outweighed, in the gravest decisions of peoples or of their leaders, by other considerations.

In proportion as civilizations are old, the richer is their history, the greater is their intellectual and artistic patrimony, and the greater, also, the accumulation of motives which may, in the opposite pan of the scale, weigh against material interests.

Is this well or ill—an advantage or a disadvantage? Let us agree that whatever makes life richer, warmer, broader and higher, cannot be an evil. The most fervent attachment to the past can be combined with a constant care for the future. If these feelings are cleared of all exclusiveness, of all narrowness, of all their negative or envious aspects, there will remain only a garland of great and fine forces.

The whole art of governing should tend to call forth the rivalry of emulation. That task has often been undertaken, and has at times succeeded.

Let us remember that in Europe, especially, problems find often a complex solution—the outcome of the atmosphere in which they were born and have developed. Into such a solution there always enter, in varying proportions, contradictory elements whose presence can be explained only by the immense network of traditions, reactions, influences and sentiments which spreads over the whole continent. At the present time this truth is found more than ever in evidence. In the course of our considerations we have tried to keep to the economic aspect of the complex problems that we have before us; but it will not be a departure from our rule, to recall in a word how the whole of international life, both political and economic, is nowadays dominated by a problem such, for instance, as that of disarmament.

Let us keep from falling into the contrary error of supposing that economic problems in Europe are thrust into the background. No; they are well in the foreground, alike in the individual concern of the various peoples and in their external relations; but their action is always complicated, and sometimes neutralized by other preoccupations.

*   *   *   *   *   *

To "the primacy of economics over politics" there is sometimes given a particular meaning different from that which we have thus far examined. In that sense, these words are understood to mean the abnormal and decisive influence that those in control of economic forces exert upon those in political power—in other words, the more or less occult dominance of men of affairs, or men of wealth, over the administrative power.

Let us be clear about it. Men who hold in their hands heavy responsibilities in the economic field cannot disinterest themselves in the general welfare. The size of the enterprises that they direct, either in industry or in finance, makes it often their duty, for their own success, to concern themselves that order should prevail in the state. When, moreover, private business reaches a high degree of extension (as is already the case with many enterprises in almost all countries), their own interests are so ramified, and cover so vast a field, that they virtually mingle with the general interests of the country itself; and so some of the leaders in such affairs come readily enough to think and to plan in terms of the public interest, even while they pursue the eventual advantage of their individual enterprise.

It is therefore legitimate, unavoidable, and desirable that the economic leaders should exercise some measure of influence upon the conduct of public affairs. But what degree? and by what means? Here the problem becomes complicated.

One rule is sure: that is, that the final decisions in public questions should be taken in complete independence by those who really and openly bear the responsibility for them. If there are influences that work separately from them, and that are strong enough to dominate their will, then "something is rotten in the state of Denmark".

To give the control of the general interests of a country into the hands of men whose thought remains dominated by purposes which, however vast, are nevertheless individual, would be an error and a danger; to give them the actual power, while leaving to others the appearances and the responsibilities, would be the worst of mistakes.

What is the truth of the matter?

Let us first clear up a confusion.

Great wealth is in itself a power. Whoever possesses it has at his disposal a force that he can turn in whatever direction pleases him. If he wishes to avail himself of it to increase his influence in public affairs, there are many methods open to him—some legitimate, some not. He can, in certain situations, have recourse to corruption, and buy up the conscience and the will of others; under other circumstances he may be able to exert, by all the modern methods for the expression of thought, a profound effect upon public opinion and consequently upon the government itself.

Men of business often have wealth at their command; but there are many exceptions to this rule. There are, on the other hand, men whose economic rôle is nothing at all, yet who have enormous wealth at their disposal.

To what then, if not to wealth itself, can be attributed the influence acquired in many such cases?

Are not the rôle and the power of a press magnate far superior to those of any banker or industrialist?

Let us here draw one first conclusion: in some cases where the appearances seem to indicate that economics are dominant over politics, it is not economics, but money, or acquired wealth, which is involved.

Furthermore, money is not the sole power to exert a pressure upon the state. Public institutions, like private enterprises, are represented and animated by men. But the reaction of these men upon each other depends fundamentally upon the personality of each; apart from any other element, the strongest personality will exert an unquestioned mastery over the others.

Let us compare the several courses—the ways which, in our modern democracies, lead to the top either of public institutions or of great private enterprises; of the two, it is sometimes the latter which demands the severer and more pitiless selection.

Even the professional peculiarities of the business man accustomed to make quick decisions, to take large and direct responsibilities, and to drive without brakes, sometimes give him at least a temporary advantage in comparison with the public man.

Indeed, the strength of particular groups arises principally out of the weakness of the central power.

But political institutions in Europe have, since the war, been passing through a grave crisis; at bottom this is the crisis of authority itself. It doubtless varies in degree, in one country and another. The parliamentary régime has been widely put to the test. Sometimes it has succumbed, sometimes it has survived only in appearance, sometimes it has held its position at the cost of more or less heavy sacrifices.

No long search need be made, to find the reason for this phenomenon.

Parliamentarism is a régime of the average, of moderation, of compromise between contradictory tendencies. In order to function, it presupposes a series of conditions—the existence of an experienced governing class, based upon a large bourgeoisie; adequate political maturity on the part of very broad sections of the electorate; the implicit acceptance, by the country as a whole, of a set of fundamental rules of action and of honor; the permanence of a certain hierarchy in the social strata, or in other terms, the absence of abrupt and total changes in the economic position of great categories of citizens; and finally, the enjoyment of a degree of culture, of history, of traditions, of material prosperity, such as to allow the government to thrive by virtue of a maximum utilization of the strength and momentum acquired.

The mere statement shows that the war, with its economic consequences, could not but have shaken that régime practically throughout Europe. In certain countries, particularly in Eastern Europe, the introduction of parliamentarism had been hasty; it existed in appearance rather than in fact, and power was actually exercised by oligarchies which were oftentimes very exclusive. In other cases, the most brilliant traditions and the best qualities of the people were such that this régime had been a " foreign body " to which the national organism had not succeeded in adapting itself.

Even in countries of a parliamentary tradition, in Western Europe, the crisis, even though not acute, is nevertheless obvious; it is a matter of concern to the parliaments themselves; it will probably lead to an internal evolution of the régime, and to an eminently desirable adaptation to the new conditions of life.

There is nothing astonishing in the fact that, with a political régime so much questioned and so little suited to ride out great storms, Europe has sometimes bent beneath the tempest since the war.

Nor is it astonishing that, upon a power often weak and lagging behind the economic evolution, powerful private interests (whatever their place in the social order, whether financiers or trade union officials) have exerted an undue pressure.

> *   *   *   *   *   *

To be just, however, we should here offer one or two reflections in extenuation of the European leaders since the war.

To begin with, the changes taking place in the technique of the production and distribution of goods have been so enormous, profound and abrupt, that they have surprised and bewildered even the professional economists. The rhythm of economic evolution, which has been accelerating for a century, was so spurred on during the war that it presents the appearance of disorder by reason of its speed. Even before 1914, it far exceeded the rhythm of evolution in political institutions. So much the more reason is there to expect today to see a separation brought about between the two. Mankind finds itself confronting new problems, which it has to solve, even if it cannot do so without delay or without damage.

And on the other hand, in the face of economic phenomena so new, of such far-reaching significance, so complex and so inescapable, it must be recognized that European opinion (or rather, Continental European opinion) is particularly ill-prepared. In the Anglo-Saxon countries, public attention has always been more attracted than elsewhere towards questions of political economy. In deliberative assemblies, in the councils of governments, and in the preoccupations of the governing classes, the economic aspect of problems has always been especially considered and emphasized.

In a great part of Europe there has long prevailed an economy with a traditional agricultural basis: that is not at all the " climate " in which the problems of modern economy germinate and grow. In the rest of Europe, where industrialization is an accomplished fact of long standing, average opinion, very conscious in those matters that concerned it directly, has often remained antagonistic or indifferent towards the broader problems presented by the world development of capitalism. The aspects of this development which have been most studied and best known are primarily those of a social or of a political order, and economics has been just a poor relation.

The task of those in power, already difficult enough in itself, was thus increased by the inadequacy of interest or support on the part of public opinion.

In conclusion, then:

Nowhere, nor at any time, have economic problems thrust themselves forward more insistently and more rigorously than in Europe since the war. Their complexity, their novelty, and their extent are the more formidable because they are superimposed upon political institutions whose foundations are either inadequate, or have been shaken. Considerations of an economic character, however, are by no means the only ones that have weight in the counsels of those in control in Europe. If it is true to say that in Europe, as elsewhere, no solution can endure if it is in direct and persistent opposition to economic interests, it is also true to repeat that in Europe, more than elsewhere, a thousand various forces sometimes come into play to neutralize economic considerations. Whoever for an instant loses sight of these primary truths cannot understand Europe after the war.

PART IV
APPLICATIONS AND CONCLUSIONS

CHAPTER VIII

BELGIUM AND THE MONETARY AND ECONOMIC CRISIS

Before bringing to a close our survey of Europe and summing up, by way of conclusion, the leading ideas which we have gathered, let us stop a while in Belgium. It is a turntable, and also, as a French economist aptly put it, " a field of experimentation." From the central standpoint that it affords, we shall look at the other side of the monetary problems which have been continually before us during these last years. The experience of Belgium will perhaps help us to see the problems a little more clearly.

Section I. Belgium and the monetary problems of the post-war period.

A.   THE GOLD STANDARD AND THE CONCENTRATION OF GOLD.

Belgium is among the countries which, relatively speaking, have the largest gold reserves. The increase of her reserve, both absolutely and relatively, has been considerable since the war.

On December 30, 1913, she held 249 millions in gold francs of the pre-war value, that is, 1,743 million francs at the present value. The financial statement of the National Bank of Belgium, issued on February 16, 1933, shows no less than 13,084 million francs in gold. The percentage of gold reserve to meet the sight obligations on December 30, 1913, was 21.60%, and on February 16, 1933, 67.23%.

In the great confusion which reigns throughout the world, in monetary as well as in other economic problems, one of the expressions most often met with, although sometimes with very different meanings, is that which complains of the maldistribution of gold throughout the world. For some the expression even carries a direct reproach against certain banks of issue.

Our first task then will be to see whether Belgium deserves this blame. We shall then see, if blame there is, whether or not someone has deserved it.

I have been at the National Bank of Belgium during two crucial periods: during the first—in the days before stabilization—our almost daily concern was to watch the gold notes leave our reserves and melt away, without, however, slowing up the depreciation of the franc on the exchange. During the second period, our anxiety was exactly the reverse. Our trouble came from a spontaneous and irresistible influx of gold notes and gold bullion into our books and vaults.

At first, naturally, we found this movement favorable, useful and necessary. Belgian capital, thanks to the stabilization, was finding its way back to the fold and returning to its normal work at home. This in a sense balanced the exaggerated movement of the other period.

But after a certain time we had the impression that the multiplication of notes put into circulation in response to this return of capital constituted a menace.

Indeed, the economic formula according to which Belgium lives is extremely delicate. We have but few natural trump cards in our hand; to defend ourselves and to live, we must be able to work under conditions which keep our cost of production at a minimum. For this reason, it is absolutely necessary for us that the cost of living remain relatively low.

Now, a rapid and excessive increase in the quantity of money in circulation, unquestionably constitutes one of the elements of a rise in prices. Undoubtedly, the rate chosen for stabilization gave us a certain breathing space. We had an exchange margin in our favor, but it was desirable that the adaptation to world prices should be as slow as possible so as to allow us to rebuild our reserves and finally to insure, for the future, the cheap living conditions from which we had benefited before the war.

This consideration was of capital importance in our eyes. For years, we have tried to employ all the traditional, regular and normal means which are at the disposition of a bank of issue, in order to hinder or retard the increase of notes in circulation. Since this increase was brought about not by an increase of our domestic holdings, but, on the contrary by a continual increase of our assets abroad and of our gold, it was to this point that we directed all our efforts.

We therefore brought our discount rate down to a level unknown for three or four decades. It came down successively, in the course of the years 1927 to 1930, from 7% to 2½% (July 31, 1930), to rise again, on January 14, 1932, to 3½%—the rate at which it has remained since then.

In the application of our regulations for the acceptance of paper at discount, we have acted in a very broad minded way, convinced as we were that in taking this stand we tended to diminish the call for capital from abroad.

For long years we have done everything in our power to prevent public organizations, or even private business, as far as we could exercise an indirect influence upon them, from borrowing abroad and thus bringing, temporarily at least, supplementary capital into Belgium.

Moreover, we have encouraged our citizens to export their capital, to take up again an interest in the international economic life—always respecting, of course, the rules which dominate these investments, among which security takes the first place.

Finally we have looked to it that no measure should be taken which would tend to attract to Belgium (for example, by facilities for investments, or guarantees against risks of exchange) capital belonging to foreigners.

But in spite of all, gold and gold monies continued to pour in upon us. To tell the truth, we were not surprised at this.

We well understood that in acting as we had done to prevent an excessive accumulation of gold, we were fulfilling a duty both national and international; our effort has not been completely wasted, in the sense that we have undoubtedly succeeded in slowing up the movement and in contracting it to a certain extent. But we were well aware that the fundamental reasons why gold and gold monies preferred to take certain directions depended no longer on monetary considerations, but on much broader considerations, primarily economic, but political and social as well.

And this is the reason why we believe that no blame can be laid at the door of the countries or the banks of issue in which gold has concentrated. They have adopted the same attitude of prudent reserve that we ourselves had taken; their reasons, perhaps, were not exactly the same as ours; however, there was one essential consideration, which held good for them as for us, and of which none of them has ever lost sight. It is this: the gold standard is an international standard; to play its part, to fulfill its function, it must be really international, that is to say it must serve a great number of countries. To accumulate gold in a few places of the globe is to compromise this essential function; but, what countries have the greatest interest, even from a personal or selfish point of view, that the gold standard remain what it was, if not the countries possessing a large gold reserve? In this way, their interest coincided with the desire to safeguard the gold standard; and this twofold consideration must have disposed them (as it has done in fact) to oppose, with all the means in their power, the accumulation of gold. I say " with all the means in their power ": we have just seen that these means were weak and insufficient, for the causes of these movements went far beyond merely monetary considerations.

May I be allowed here to recall a comparison which is not new but which yet seems to me very apt. Gold, in banks of issue, is like the mercury in a thermometer. What is the use of getting angry when you see the mercury rise to indicate temperatures of 70 or 80 degrees? You may well try to hold it down, to change it, to replace it; if you have not changed the temperature of the room, the mercury will go up again, expand, and always register the same. So it is with the gold in the banks of issue. Try as you will to redistribute it, as the favorite expression goes, if you have not changed the fundamental monetary and political causes which have brought about the present concentration, it will be labor lost.

B. THE GOLD EXCHANGE STANDARD.

At this point I hear an objection which has become current. " If all the countries in the world were to establish a metallic reserve even far below the 67% of which we spoke just now for Belgium, all the gold at the disposal of mankind would not suffice. The mere attempt would bring about a run on gold which would make it scarce; prices would continue to fall to a level at which the existing system would be in danger of collapse. Then even under the best conditions there must needs be recourse to the gold exchange standard. This gold exchange standard, however, has lent itself in the course of this recent period to such abuses that it has appeared, for awhile, as the scapegoat for the crisis. You yourselves, in Belgium, have completely abandoned it."

It is true that at this moment we are on the gold bullion standard pure and simple; but the road by which we have come to it is well worth describing.

Belgium was one of the first countries of Western Europe to put into practice a sort of mixed gold exchange standard. As early as 1870, the directors of the National Bank accepted, as part of their metallic reserve, foreign drafts which carried a special provision for payment in gold.

On several occasions, this system was put to practical test, that is to say, the agreements for rediscount and the provisions for payment in gold were brought into play, to make sure that they would work normally. One of these experiments took place during the crisis of 1907; it was entirely conclusive in a favorable sense.

After the war, the gold exchange system had an extraordinary popularity. When, in the course of the years 1924-25, a great effort was made under the leadership of the Bank of England to reestablish order in the monetary systems of Europe, and to stabilize the different currencies on the gold basis, recourse to the gold exchange standard appeared to be a healthy and necessary method.

One of the bases for stabilization operations consisted in the conclusion of a loan in gold notes; the certificates in fact remained invested on the lending market; they became part of the reserves of the central bank of the borrowing country; these reserves thus reached the level that was judged necessary to give confidence and to offset the normal fluctuations in the balance of payments. The method permitted the loaning market to lend more easily, and the borrowers to find a partial compensation, practically indispensable, for the charges of the loan.

Belgium followed the same course; the loan which she contracted, on the principal markets paying in gold, was made under very burdensome conditions. It was understood from the beginning that the National Bank of Belgium would endeavor to realize, on the sums thus put at its disposal, compensatory interest, which was counted upon as a normal return.

The greater part of these returns benefited the State and lightened for it the charges on the loan for stabilization.

I am well aware of the dangers and drawbacks of such a system; I continue to believe, however, that the advantages far outweigh the disadvantages, and that a little good will and a reasonable understanding of the interests of both sides would be sufficient to make the system function under conditions from which the more serious drawbacks would be excluded.

Moreover, if the gold exchange standard had been applied only in the particular case of monetary stabilization, and if, on the other hand, the rules which are at the very base of its functioning had not been violated, it is very probable that the abuses which we have seen developed, and from which we have suffered, would never have arisen. Indeed, the gold exchange standard presupposes a weaker market leaning on a stronger market which functions as its center. The first conclusion to be drawn from this is that the central market must itself be a true center and that it must not, in its turn, count on the support of another market. Then there must be, between the assisted market and the central market, a difference of such importance that the latter can, without being shaken to its foundations, bear the changes (even sudden and profound) which may occur in the situation of the former. This really means in practice that only the small markets should have recourse to the gold exchange standard; the great centers themselves should desist from employing it;

in any case, what should be absolutely prohibited are such reciprocal relations as involve the use of the methods of the gold exchange standard between two great markets called upon to play their part as centers. It is in this that the principal danger of the system really lies—namely, the artificial creation of piled-up credits, a creation which prevents the normal and necessary reactions of a true gold standard.

Belgium is a small market; the considerations which we have just discussed were weighed and appraised there, but they did not concern us directly.

We had distributed our credits in notes on the various large markets paying in gold, which in view of their absolute and traditional importance we considered as true gold centers. The volume of deposits and assets which the National Bank of Belgium maintained on each of these markets was so small in proportion to the power of these markets that it was certainly not of a nature, in any circumstances, to cause them any serious trouble or to involve them in any reactions contrary to their particular interests.

Under these conditions, there was, as far as we were concerned, no objection of an international kind to our pursuing a policy which afforded us indisputable advantages, particularly valuable in view of our burdens.

However, we have never remained insensible to considerations of a general nature; we have always realized that no country can isolate itself, or follow solely its own interests, or avoid the reactions which a general trend exercises, even though indirectly, on its situation. We were concerned therefore with the difficulties or dangers inherent in practices of which we were aware and which seemed to us abuses. In consequence, we have sought for a position we could take without sacrificing our own interests, while at the same time playing a useful part in the international game.

These are the main points of the position which we have chosen.

First of all we have insisted on reducing, as far as was compatible with the charges of our stabilization loan, our recourse to the gold exchange standard. We have determined to employ a mixed system comprising a proportion of gold bullion, corresponding to the 40% which is imposed on us by law as a cover, and to leave only the surplus in the form of foreign monies, considering them as a security margin. In this way we reduced for ourselves the danger—very remote at that moment—which the possession of assets in foreign currencies might hold in store for us. At the same time, we were taking our share of the burden which is inherent in the holding of an inactive gold reserve, a burden which certain banks of issue found too heavy for them at that moment.

In dealing with our external funds which were thus reduced, we were more careful than ever to avoid everything which might have rendered more difficult the task of the bank of issue on the central market. First of all, we took care to distribute them more equally among the various markets paying in gold. On each particular market, in London, New York, and Paris, we insisted on working in perfect agreement with the bank of issue, and we concentrated in the hands of that institution itself the major portion of our assets —a policy which sometimes meant for us a noticeable reduction of interest.

When we had to change from one currency to another, we avoided any operation which might weigh on the exchange rates at a moment of difficulty; thus we have never left one market for another except at times when the currency which we were selling was the stronger one and that which we were buying the weaker one. In this way our action corresponded to the interest of the markets concerned; we relieved one market and strengthened the other.

I really believe that even by examining our books with the magnifying glass, it would be impossible to find a single case in which we acted in contradiction to the rule which I have just stated.

This was particularly true of our attitude towards England, even when rumors began to spread uneasiness concerning the pound sterling.

Indeed, our position was extremely difficult We had always had very considerable credits on the London market. This is easily understood. London has always been and still is, on the whole, the most complete and important monetary and financial center in the world.

Deeply convinced as we were of the necessity for well organized international commercial relations based on a common standard, we believed that we had a real, although indirect, interest in not undermining the rôle of primary importance played by London in the financing of world economy.

The English market was one of our principal customers, and the relations between Belgian business and English finance have been uninterrupted. On our Stock Exchange, the currency which for years had been most dealt in and most sought after was the pound sterling.

Moreover, the London market had taken a portion of the stabilization loan concluded by Belgium in 1926, and we had left the proceeds from it on the market.

All these reasons induced us to desire the strengthening of the London exchange. They were not sufficient, however, to relieve our very real apprehensions, such as the strain on the pound created the world over.

We therefore decided on a compromise which, while permitting us on the one hand to take the precautions imposed on us in the interest of our country, did not, on the other hand, weaken, by a selfish attitude, the position of London.

We determined to continue the policy which I have described above, that is, to replace external assets by gold bullion in our reserve, and to redistribute more equitably or more equally our assets on the various gold markets. But, applying more strictly than ever the rules which I have stated above, we took care not to sell a single pound at a moment when pressure was being exerted against this currency on the exchange.

Thus when things were precipitated, and particularly in the last days when the panic increased on all the markets in the world, we deliberately chose not to sell a single pound.

When the suspension of the gold exchange standard was decreed, on September 21, 1931, we still had, on the London market, 12,600,000 pounds belonging " *en nue-propriété* " to the National Bank of Belgium.

Certainly, these pounds were not without a sort of indirect guarantee. Indeed, we had taken care that the amount of our claims in pounds should not be inferior to the total sum which Belgium owed England in pounds on account of various loans, and especially on account of the English portion of the stabilization loan.

The National Bank, which in all this question acted only with an eye to the general interests, had long before taken care to come to an understanding on this subject with the Treasury, which received the largest part of the returns on these investments in pounds.

Yet, in deciding to leave in London a part of our credits in pounds, we accepted a real burden. The National Bank of Belgium thus exposed itself to difficulties and attacks which the event soon proved to be a disagreeable reality.

This sacrifice (because, within these limits, there had really been a sacrifice) had been deliberate; it was accepted for the sake of the gold standard and the international cooperation of the economic markets.

But, when the news reached us of the English default, we knew that the gold exchange standard had received a heavy blow. To persist in this policy would have been in our opinion to run new risks for a cause already lost. Loyally and courageously we had applied up to the end the rules of international cooperation in monetary affairs; but it seemed to us that we had reached the end, since the principal protagonists had withdrawn from the game. Nothing remained for us but to take decisive measures, considering only our own interests.

On that very day, therefore, we determined to give up the gold exchange standard and to go over completely to the system of the gold bullion standard. We asked all our correspondents and particularly the central banks to bring into play the facilities which they had promised us, and to give effect to the engagements assumed toward us. Within a few days, the cover backing our notes was composed entirely of gold bullion.

C. COOPERATION AMONG CENTRAL BANKS.

The very frank account which I have just given makes it evident that we have remained faithful, through all vicissitudes, to the policy of cooperation among banks of issue. We benefited from this policy at a certain time in our monetary history, when we brought about stabilization in 1926. Since then, we have not ceased to take our share, on every occasion, in the common effort which was required of the stronger in the interest of the others.

We have taken part every time when a collective action of the banks of issue has been organized. Sometimes, indeed, the part which we undertook was relatively very heavy, and was greater than that which should have fallen to us if only the resources of the central banks concerned had been taken into consideration. I shall only cite, in order to make the point clear, the opening of discount credits made to the National Banks of Austria, of Hungary, of Rumania, of Poland, of Italy, etc. . . .

As far as the Bank for International Settlements is concerned, our attitude has been the same; we have taken a share of the capital of the Bank equal to that of the chief banks of issue, and we have made a special effort to place its bonds on our market.

In the various operations which have been carried on recently under the auspices of the Bank for International Settlements, we have insisted on doing all that was expected of us, even in cases when we sometimes wondered whether the policy followed was really the best.

If we have adhered so faithfully to this policy, in spite of the surprises which it has sometimes held in store for us, and in spite of the efforts it required of us, it is because we were convinced that it was absolutely indispensable. Recent events, and particularly the reactions of the depression, have only confirmed us more strongly in this conviction. It is impossible that international economic relations should continue and develop normally if they cannot rely on regular conditions of international financing. For this an international standard must exist and play its part satisfactorily. Anything which compromises the international monetary system compromises international economic life.

Section II. The position of the belga.

It was said before that there is at present no actual monetary problem in Belgium. Let us examine the situation in this respect.

A. TECHNICAL POSITION.

None of the causes of weakness, none of the dangers which can threaten a currency, is found upon analysis in the situation of the belga.

First of all, from an intrinsic point of view, its position is exceedingly strong.

The reserves which guarantee the sight liabilities are composed exclusively of gold bullion. The relation of the metallic cover to the total liabilities—notes and current accounts—in the course of the year has fluctuated between 65% and 69%, according to the official publications of the Bank; but everyone knows that banks of issue usually keep in their tills a supplementary reserve which permits them to face more easily and more discreetly the first attacks in case of a possible run. We naturally do not want to make an exception to this rule, and because of this our position is still stronger than it appears to be.

This gold reserve is not burdened with the indirect mortgage that is constituted by having considerable foreign funds invested in the country. In fact, contrary to what is the case among several of our neighbours, foreign capital deposited with us does not (thanks perhaps to the measures which we have tried to take) reach a very large sum;—in truth, this sum is quite insignificant in relation to our economic power and our reserves.

To complete the picture, I must recognize, however, that the credits contracted abroad in recent months have brought to our doors an influx of gold which must some day leave the country again.

As regards long-term loans, the problem may be said not to exist; there is, however, an undeniable one in the case of short-term loans. But the total of loans of this character contracted by Belgium abroad is of so little importance in proportion to our gold assets, that it is negligible from the point of view which we are discussing.

Moreover, it is a part of the programme of the Belgian Government to consolidate the Treasury certificates floated abroad. That is what it has actually done, recently, for a considerable sum and under conditions so favorable as to permit the belief that it will have no difficulty in accomplishing the consolidation of the other certificates still remaining on a short-term basis outside of the country.

Another interesting technical element is constituted by the funds invested abroad, and possessed by Belgians.

Our fellow-countrymen have not been too seriously affected by the measures which have blocked capital abroad, in Europe and outside of Europe. Undoubtedly, the sum total of the funds thus immobilized is not without importance; doubtless too, the effects of this blocking involve for a considerable number of firms individual difficulties which are serious and sometimes tragic. On the whole, however, that amount (whether it concerns investments of a financial character or sums proceeding from current commercial operations) is not such as to create among us reactions that might shake our exchange.

As to the discount portfolio of the National Bank of Belgium, it is still, at the present time, in spite of the strain put on us by the depression, considerably less (taking into account the present value of the franc) than it was just before the war at a time when the situation was considered normal.

The total circulation—notes and current liabilities—has clearly reached a more or less stable level. The figures have not changed appreciably since October 15, 1931. They have, since that date, fluctuated around the figure of 19 billion francs.

If you try to figure per capita the amount of means of payment in circulation, you find that, expressed in gold, the increase relative to the pre-war period is smaller for our country than for several of our neighbors, whereas their economic situation is very much the same as ours.

As for the foreign exchange market in Belgium, it is absolutely free. The National Bank, indeed, has a foreign exchange service. It deals on the stock market for its individual clients. It intervenes also, at certain times, to reduce the excessive fluctuations of quotations, either by selling or by taking up foreign monies. We do not lose sight of the fact that the scope of the exchange market, in spite of the economic importance of our country, is relatively small, and that at certain periods, if we did not interfere, sudden fluctuations might occur in the gold points—fluctuations the extent of which would be in the interest neither of Belgian commerce nor of its counterpart abroad.

But the National Bank has taken as a guiding policy in this matter an attitude of complete reserve, and has determined to intervene only when the private banks have exhausted all their possibilities and employed all their proper facilities. In this way we have succeeded in developing a very active and flexible foreign exchange market entirely independent of us, which is capable of supporting itself in most cases and in practically all the ordinary circumstances of business life.

Finally, as regards the movements of gold over our counters, we adopted, two and a half years ago (i. e., on August 1, 1930), a rule which we have not since modified. We accept or release gold indifferently under the terms of our regulation; in other words, we completely and strictly apply the rules inherent in the automatic functioning of the gold bullion standard.

It would in short, from a purely technical point of view, be hard to find any weakness in our monetary system, or any danger that could in greater or less degree threaten the stability of the belga in relation to gold.

B. SITUATION OF THE BUDGET AND THE NATIONAL ECONOMY.

But manifestly it is not technical questions alone which count, and a currency may sometimes be involved in serious difficulties through outside influences.

Of such influences, we shall discuss two kinds: some have

their origin in budgetary difficulties, others in the general economic situation of the country. We shall intentionally limit ourselves to those, and leave aside the external aspects of the problem, because throughout this study we have taken a purely Belgian point of view.

1. *Budget.*

However strong the technical position of a currency may be, it is certain that a continuous series of budgets with heavy deficits presents most serious dangers. Indeed, the lack of normal revenue will force the State to have recourse to extraordinary remedies. It will first turn to loans. But supposing that these deficits repeat themselves and reach considerable amounts, the capital market will soon be closed to it, whether because of weariness, of exhaustion or of lack of confidence. From that moment, there will be no other way than direct or indirect recourse to the printing press—that is, to straight inflation.

But the bank of issue, in Belgium, is particularly well equipped in this respect. Not only is the treasury of the Bank (a stockholding company), independent of the treasury of the State, but the amount of National Government bonds which the Bank can own at any time is narrowly limited: it is only a hundred millions.

There is, then, no immediate danger. But one must always take into account psychological elements.

Let us not forget that, after the disastrous experiences undergone since the war, public opinion, in a general way, is much more sensitive than before to all the events which relate to monetary stability; it reacts much more quickly and much more impulsively; a flight from the currency would be much more rapid, more extensive, and harder to check than it has been before.

It might be that, leaving aside positive elements, the mere fact of persistent budgetary disequilibrium would set into motion reactions of a psychological nature, and that a dangerous strain might result. Where do we stand in this respect?

In Belgium, after the years of great budgetary prosperity

following the stabilization of 1926, the years of difficulty have come: the budget of 1930 had a deficit of francs 1,200,-000,000; that of 1931, of 1,523,000,000; that of 1932, of 2,260,000,000 (estimated figures).

Happily, important Treasury reserves had been earlier built up; in April, 1930, they amounted to about 5 billions. One part of them was devoted to the anticipatory redemption of securities of the foreign debt. When the balance of it had been used up, the Government, in 1931 and 1932, had recourse to borrowing. In the second half of 1932, serious apprehensions began to make themselves felt and to penetrate to the public. It was understood that it was not possible to continue placing loans in the same rapid succession; and that, if serious surprises were to be avoided, normal expenses and income had to be balanced.

A great effort was made. The budget for 1933, which the Government has just proposed, is balanced; it even leaves a slight surplus.

This equilibrium has been reached more through an increase in taxes than through a reduction of expenses.

The statement of the basis for the budget estimates the new taxes at 1,450,000,000 francs and the reduction of expenses, as compared with 1932, at about 1,000,000,000.

It is fair to recognize that the country has made a great effort; the total burden of taxes has reached (if not exceeded) the point where it threatens to become a danger to the productive capacity of our economic system.

There are many good minds who estimate that a more drastic reduction is indispensable if the international economic situation of Belgium is to be insured for the future. This is a consideration which, although very important in itself, lies outside the realm of our discussion. Indeed, even if the total burden of the budget is too heavy for the economy of a country, the difficulties will only make themselves felt at a distant date, it may even be that they will not arise, or will not clearly manifest themselves, before another crisis. In any case, as the Treasury is now insured, any menace of a monetary kind disappears, and we are therefore warranted in re-

affirming the confidence with which the position of the belga
has inspired us.

2. *National Economy.*

It might be said that a currency would lie under a threat,
far-off and indirect, but serious, if the fundamental conditions of the economic system that employs it were vitiated.
In other words, if a country found itself in a fundamentally
bad economic situation, this condition would, in the end,
react on the monetary situation.

But we may well declare that the economic situation of
Belgium at this time is still, in a general way, one of the least
unfavorable in the whole world. No doubt, we are badly hit
by the depression. All the manifestations of our economic
activity are in a noticeable decline. We face, as do so many
others, a serious problem of unemployment; our producers
are daily struggling against extreme difficulties. But in
spite of all this, we may, when we look around us, still consider ourselves to be in a comparatively fortunate position.

Our foreign trade still represents, in comparison with its
gold value of 1927, 56.4% for imports and 56.7% for exports, whereas these same figures respectively are, for Germany, 32.8% and 56.1%; for France, 56.2% and 35.7%;
for the United States, 31.7% and 34%.

The total of those completely unemployed, in relation to
the insured or affiliated working population, was, in December last, 18.65% in Belgium, while at that time it reached
45.1% in Germany, and, in November, 34% in the United
States.

The number of failures certainly has increased, but to a
moderate extent. None of the very large banks, and no very
large business concern in our country, has had a spectacular
collapse. In 1932, the total deposits in the "Caisse Générale
d'Epargne et de Retraite" and in the "Caisse Centrale de
Crédit du Boerenbond" represented, respectively, 286% and
172% of the figures for 1927.

Ask anyone who has travelled in Belgium: all the external
indications which have impressed him will show that our

10

country has stood the storm of the crisis better than most
other countries.

*   *   *   *   *   *

The conclusion is almost a paradox. We find ourselves
undeniably confronted by a crisis, the most indisputable characteristic of which is its universality; it extends into all fields,
it strikes all countries, whatever their régime; it is essentially
international.

Because of Belgium's very constitution, her lack of natural
resources, her geographical position, and her traditions, she
is a country very closely dependent upon international conditions; and in spite of this, she has held out better than the
countries which have tried to protect themselves by the most
radical measures of economic nationalism.

Why? I see only one explanation: it is that the Belgians
have respected more faithfully than many others the rules of
international monetary and economic relations.

On this account, our economic system has felt earlier and
more quickly the reactions of the international situation. It has
maintained a greater flexibility, a larger capacity for adaptation. The important executives of our industry, as well as the
Belgian working class, follow very closely the exigencies of
the international situation, and consent more easily to the
sacrifices necessary to allow the indispensable adjustments.
By continuing to practice a liberal policy in regard to tariffs
and exchanges, we have kept the cost of living relatively low.

Thus, the working class has accepted very early, and very
wisely, the wage reductions made necessary by the fall in
prices; on the other hand, heavy industry had, in the days of
prosperity, built up reserves which are very precious now.
Finally, there has been maintained among us a middle sized
industry, well in hand and well directed, which has known
how to turn around, and change its methods, its processes of
manufacture and its outlets, with remarkable flexibility.

In a word, if Belgium suffers less than others now, it is
because she has earlier had the courage to consent to the
sacrifices demanded by the falling cyclical curve; and if she
has been able to do this, if she has been able to impose these

sacrifices on her people, it is because she has in a large measure remained faithful to the rules of an adequate international intercourse.

And so we are brought back to our starting point, that is to the necessity for international action to solve the whole body of problems forced upon us by the crisis.

On this capital point, public opinion has unanimously upheld the Belgian Government, and has not changed its attitude.

The opinion expressed on this subject by the Geneva experts, in their annotated project for the programme of the coming World Conference, corresponds exactly to the prevailing sentiment in Belgium.

CHAPTER IX

GENERAL CONCLUSIONS

The balance of so many errors, gropings and contradictions, superimposed upon that of the crisis, could not fail to be disastrous. Each item of it bears witness to a formidable deficit: —in the economic field, production reduced by half, exchanges two-thirds paralyzed; in the social field, unemployment among tens of millions, generations being brought up without work, proletarianization, or social dismay of growing sections of the people; in the moral field, the breaking down of respect for obligations, and, above all, the enfeebling of the ideas of justice and of responsibility, beneath the blows of undeserved but inevitable misfortunes.

Confronting a great disaster, men always seek, by a natural impulse, to fix the blame for it. They have not failed to do so in this case.

But to what end? One casts the blame upon the other; and the only result is to distract attention and energies which should be devoted altogether to the struggle against the crisis.

Doubtless, if one examines the particular position of one or another state, and the conditions in which it was led to adopt the decisions criticized, one will often find an explanation of its attitude. Sometimes it has been driven to it in order to avoid greater evils. In certain cases, it has found itself led to react against like measures taken by its neighbors. Often, too, it has been dragged in by circumstances that were beyond its possibilities of isolated action, drifted by currents that engulfed it along with a hundred others, and without other means of resistance because of the lack of any genuine international collaboration. Thus a whole series of provisions which, looked at from above and set as parts into a framework, are blameworthy and harmful, are to be found individually explainable, and in some degree subjectively justified.

135

It should even be said that three or four European countries have shown, in those fields depending exclusively on them, an unusual energy, for example in the matter of budgetary equilibrium. But many others have to reproach themselves with serious failures, for which they can blame no one but themselves. Before an international effort can be helpful to them, each of them must gather its national energies, look into its own conscience, and begin by putting its own house in order.

In truth, all peoples without exception bear a share of the responsibility in the common misery. All must give their help to the task of international restoration, and assume their share of the sacrifices.

It is perhaps to be regretted that the crisis, which was to strike all peoples, did not fall upon them all at about the same time. Certain great countries believed for a long while that they would escape the torment, and remain immune amidst disasters that struck the others. Harsh experience has shown them the vanity of this hope. But meanwhile, this state of mind had acted as an obstacle to the development of any action in common.

However that may be, the important thing is not to determine the immediate reasons which have caused leaders to take one decision instead of another, but rather to go back to the deeper causes that made such an attitude, at a given moment, inevitable.

Many of the criticisms that one hears formulated remain without meaning and without result because they are directed towards the effects rather than towards the causes.

Thus most of the complaints that used to be made against the operations of monetary stabilization which effected a devalorization were, in fact, deserved not by the stabilization itself, but by the inflation that had made it inevitable.

Similarly, many criticisms that are made of the standstill agreements concern the excesses and the common errors which brought about a situation from which there was no other issue than the conclusion of such agreements.

How many complaints we have heard, during these recent

years, about the general spread of distrust, about the necessity of reviving, among the investing public, the tendency towards long-term investments, etc. On all the evidence, that is putting the cart before the horse; after the cruel experiences that the great public has had, it will make up its mind to resume a constructive attitude when order is reestablished, and not before.

The manifestations of economic nationalism, of which we have studied some of the forms to be found in the recent situation in Europe, represent only one of those deeper currents of ideas and of facts, in the development of which all the peoples of the world share alike the responsibility.

Here we should point out, with particular emphasis, the evil influence exerted upon the practical development of economic nationalism by the abuses which have crept in and little by little become prevalent in international competition, whether or not supported by governmental action.

Dumping, in all its forms—sale at prices below the cost of production, export premiums, shipping subsidies, reduction of transportation tariffs, transshipment surtaxes,—introduced into international economic relations an element of disorder which prevented the natural correctives from coming into play, and which made practically inevitable measures of retaliation of a more and more artificial character.

*　*　*　*　*　*

But whoever may be responsible and whatever may be the causes of the misfortune, it is on our backs. Coming to the conclusion of our study, we are led to put a finger upon the critical point, following after the series of immediate manifestations, in which are summed up the gravest difficulties of the crisis—the fall in prices.

We need not take up here the analysis which has often been made the subject of special studies, to explain how and why prices first soared to excessively high levels, only to go down again to the extremely low figures at which we find them now. Nor will we refer further to the process of the decrease of prices; we shall not analyze the way in which it disorganizes the mechanism of production, nor its repercussions upon the respective positions of the various social classes. We shall content ourselves with taking up the facts as they present themselves to our eyes today; we shall thus set into relief one of the fundamental effects of the fall in prices upon the relations between creditors and debtors, taking the two words in the largest sense, so as to extend it to all those who have to pay or to receive, by virtue of contracts, fixed sums expressed in monetary units.

At the present level of wholesale prices, the hiatus between the juridical position of the creditors and the actual capacity of the debtors is such that many agreements are no longer carried out in full.

While, on the one hand, the claims remain fixed at the same number of monetary units, the purchasing power of each of these units has been theoretically increased; on the other hand, real estate, movable property, and stocks, are represented by amounts reduced in terms of monetary units. The command that the creditors have over goods is therefore increased as prices fall. This fact is the more marked in the case of long-term credits.

But on the whole, the amortization and interest service on loans in general can be effected only by means of the actual wealth produced by the efforts of manufacturers and laborers, utilizing the capital invested; there must be production, to assure satisfaction of the rights of the creditors.

So, then, even if the debt charge burdening the instruments of production had remained the same—even if it had not been made heavier in its actual incidence by the fall of prices, the dwindling of economic activity would have made it a material difficulty to continue at the full rates the service of the loans.

But at the present time, the two elements combine to render more inextricable the respective positions of the debtors and of the creditors. All over the world, the means of production are partially paralyzed; the reduction in national revenues undergone during the last three years is estimated at forty or even fifty percent and the general indebtedness, already raised to an excessive level during the boom, has become an intolerable burden under the pressure of lowered prices.

And so we find ourselves in a dilemma. Either prices must go up or credits must be readjusted and adapted to the actual price level. Whether this adaptation be made in the form of a reduction of interest, of a suspension or postponement of amortizations, or of a scaling down of principal, the result is in any case a reduction of the actual charge.

The maintenance of a sufficient degree of stability in prices is the necessary condition for continuous economic progress and even more for the preservation of a permanent social order. Inflation and deflation are both hurtful. Any sudden or profound modification in the value of the currency (that is, in prices) defeats the real execution of contracts, and in consequence does violence alike to the intentions of the parties, to equity, and to the social order.

By inflation, it is the creditor elements that are deprived of their legitimate rights, for the benefit of other categories who have possessions in real values. In deflation, the inverse form of injustice results; it is the creditors who receive or who claim more than they have actually given.

But the rise and the fall of prices must be differently judged. A moderate, slow and continuous rise of prices is, in practice, an element of prosperity; it permits of the automatic correction of the inevitable mistakes made by producers and by intermediaries; it acts like oil in the bearings of a machine. By favoring the development of production, and aiding active elements, it affords the creditors a guarantee for the complete execution of the obligations undertaken towards them; and besides, by raising interest rates, it furnishes them a compensation for the slight diminution in the purchasing power of their claims.

A fall of prices, on the contrary, is always identified with a period of economic difficulties. It should, apparently, be accompanied by an improvement in the situation of the creditors; but as a matter of fact, the resulting diminution of activity is necessarily accompanied by a reduction of the advantages actually reaped by them.

In theory, the general level of prices at which an equilibrium is finally established is of no importance. Provided that there is harmony among the different factors of the economy—that labor is employed, that capital is at work, that the factories are busy, that debts are duly proportionate to the actual earnings of industry—it is of little enough importance whether the equilibrium be found at one level or another.

But in practice, when (as has been the case this time) the fall has been great and unrelieved, the effort of general adaptation that must be made in order to get back to a given level of prices is so difficult and so dangerous that it is sometimes better to give up the effort to do so entirely, and seek to raise this level before stabilizing it with a view to making it the basis of a new order.

Attention has often been drawn to the effects upon wages, and upon the relations between employers and employees, of a deflation carried too far. Let us here confine ourselves to recalling the actual factors, in a period of deflation, of the relations of creditors to debtors.

The position of the creditors, who have their rights expressed in monetary units, is unassailable from the juridical point of view. They forego enforcing the validity of their rights only when they find themselves confronting an absolute material impossibility. But the network of rights is infinitely complex; there are numerous creditors who are at the same time debtors, as are the banks, for instance; they cannot forego insisting upon their rights in full, unless they themselves obtain from their own creditors concessions equivalent to those that they are led to make to their debtors.

But when both creditors and debtors arrive at the point of a default—at a point where fulfillment is a material impossibility—they must needs yield. The adjustment is then made often by the most detestable means, that is, by bankruptcy, by default, by the unilateral suspension of the obligations assumed. Thus comes about the cascade of losses extending from the producers to the banks, from the banks to the depositors and to the lenders of all categories.

Surely there is a period, in the descent of the cyclical curve, where the lowering of prices is the necessary reaction to the excesses of the boom. It then brings, and should bring, a cleansing of the economic organism, ridding it of its parasites and of its excrescences; liquidations, which are the penalty paid for the excesses committed, should then be made, and the sooner the better. But there comes a moment when the equilibrium is upset again in the opposite direction, and healthy going enterprises find themselves threatened. The general prevalence of defaults in payments shows that there is a profound derangement in the very mechanism of business. This is the point at which the problem we are considering presents itself.

Experience has cruelly confirmed the truth of these deductions. If there were to be drawn up today an account of the credits that are either lost or overdue or compromised, the total would be enormous—depositors deprived of their accounts, banks involved in the difficulties of their clients, mortgage creditors reduced to impotence, bondholders unpaid, and so on.

The situation is no less serious within the frontiers in a number of countries (in the United States, for instance) than in international financial relations.

Let us pause a moment on this latter aspect of the problem, in Europe.

The foreign debt, for a whole series of European countries, has become formidably heavy, whether one compares it to the whole public debt, or to the export capacity of the country, or to its fiscal resources.

In certain cases, it mounts up to sums that preclude any possibility of a full execution at the prevailing price level.

There are some cases in which this debt, even if we were living in normal times, would of itself be genuinely excessive. This evil is due alike to the leaders of the country, who have not been willing or able to see clearly, and to the foreign financiers who have literally dragged them into this course by imprudent persuasions and by blind complaisance.

We will say no more on the subject of the mistakes made in the excessive granting of short-term credits, and the serious troubles that have resulted from it.

But let us point out that, for many European countries, the

capacity of payment abroad depends fundamentally both
upon their opportunities for exportation and upon the price
that they can obtain for their products.

The problem has two aspects: for one thing, it is of a
general character, and dominated by relations that go beyond
the particular will of the debtors as well as of the creditors;
for another, it is temporary in the sense that any modification
in the general situation of Europe, or in the level of prices,
will have direct influences upon its solution.

It is unquestionably necessary to maintain strictly the
sacred and absolute character of obligations assumed. The
general rules of law and of equity should be applied in full,
both as to the liabilities of the debtor and as to his eventual
discharge of them. But while the principles remain intact,
it is to the common interest of the parties to see the facts in
their reality, and to limit losses as strictly as possible.

It has been suggested in various quarters that there should
be designated, under the auspices of some international institution, some individuals of the highest type, who would be
requested to act in the capacity of friendly mediators between
debtor states and foreign creditors. It would be understood
that the formation of this group would not in any respect
limit the absolute liberty of the parties either in their choice
of methods or in the decisions to be made, and that its intervention would occur only on the express demand of both
parties.

Even when presented with these reservations and qualifi-
cations, the suggestion has aroused many objections, so great
is the fear of seeing any pressure—even indirect, even remote
—exerted upon the will of the creditors, to the detriment of
their interests.

Yet it would seem that a *rapprochement,* under impartial
auspices, would be useful in many cases to both parties. The
creditors are often in no position, through lack of organization, to see where their material interest lies, and to consent
in time to concessions which would, in the end, be genuine
measures of conservation. On the other hand, in a situation

such as that of the present time, hasty decisions or definitive concessions would be as inappropriate as a stubborn ignorance.

However that may be, let us repeat once more that the foreign creditors, if they wish their claims to be paid in full, must make it possible for their debtors to export their products and services in sufficient volume and at normal prices. There is no other alternative.

*   *   *   *   *   *

All things considered, the creditors have the same interest as the debtors in seeing prices raised, so as to find stability again at a level which makes easier all the necessary adaptations. Wisdom will no doubt dictate, and necessity will probably compel, recourse to these two methods: agreements will be effected for the purpose of regulating, sometimes definitively, sometimes temporarily, the position of certain categories of debtors who are in especial difficulties; and meanwhile, a readjustment of prices incidentally to the alleviation of the crisis, and the resumption of economic activity, will bring about the solution of the problem.

But this is only a hope, or an end. Just what can be done to facilitate or to make possible the raising of prices?

On this point, the most authoritative counsels are divided; they attach themselves to one or to the other of two theories which are in violent opposition.

Prices represent a relationship between money and goods. They are affected in two ways by the law of supply and demand; they may be influenced, on the one hand, by all the variations which take place in the supply or in the demand for goods; and on the other hand, by all the variations which may be brought about in the supply and in the demand for money.

Of course "money" must be understood in the broadest sense of the word, including therein not only currency but also credit currency.

Innumerable proposals have been put forward with a view to changing prices by means of monetary manipulations; we cannot agree with any of these which lead either directly or indirectly to the issuance of currency arbitrarily, without an immediate and sure economic basis, and so to speak in the air.

It is, in our opinion, not the scarcity of monetary facilities or of credit that has loosed the present crisis upon us; it seems to us more reasonable to believe, on the contrary, that the excess of stock exchange loans, over-capitalization, the abuses of the gold exchange standard, and a hundred other unjustified or ill-proportioned forms of credit, by pushing prices and quotations to excessive levels, brought about a reaction, and thus contributed to the origin of the crisis. The experiments that have been made during the course of the crisis, tending to multiply currency for the purpose of increasing the purchasing power of the public, have led so far to no result; the increase in the quantity of money put into circulation has been counter-balanced by a decrease in the velocity of circulation.

For some time there has been agitated in certain quarters a project for the simultaneous devalorization of all the currencies in relation to the old gold standard; they would reduce the quantity of gold contained in each monetary unit, simultaneously in all countries.

But such a measure would not of itself change at all the essential problem of prices nor consequently that of the relations between debtors and creditors.

In effect, this vast devaluation would act upon prices only if it resulted in the multiplication of fiduciary issues based on gold. But there is no reason to judge that these new issues would find grounds for their emission, or that, once made, they would be absorbed into circulation, and would not themselves be neutralized by the diminution of the velocity of circulation.

Recourse to a general devaluation would appear useful only if the actual basis on which the monetary edifice rests were too narrow; but we believe that that is not at all the case. The real problem presented by the gold standard does not lie in the greater or less extension of the metallic basis, but rather, indeed, in the form, the size, the solidity and the elasticity of the monetary and credit superstructure to be built upon this basis.

Doubtless the mere fact of taking an attitude of an inflationist tendency, and doing so by an international decision, might have an effect upon the public mind, and lead to reactions of a psychological sort which would perhaps be sufficient to set in movement, at least temporarily, an upward movement of prices. But we are firmly convinced that such a movement, if it were supported by nothing else, would be bound to encounter the same obstacles as now exist, would soon have its wings clipped; and the reaction of the public, after a new disappointment, would be in danger of accentuating further the gravity of the previous situation.

In short, we will discard as inadequate, and as dangerous, those solutions which approach the problem of prices from the angle of monetary manipulations.

Even supposing that solutions of this character were to be successful in raising prices, and giving the fillip that would get us out of the vicious circle of prices, it would nevertheless be well to reflect twice before having recourse to it. That is a slope on which it is difficult to stop, when once a slide has begun. The precedent would involve a risk of upsetting, even more than they have been already, those ideas upon which the whole organization of credit rests.

Does that mean that there is no fundamental monetary question which it is urgent to solve? Certainly not. But in our opinion, the problem of prices must be approached from another angle—from the side of the movement of goods, or at any rate in correlation with it.

An international monetary regime cannot be effective nor can it continue, if it does not correspond with an international exchange of capital and of products. Whatever may be the solution given to the monetary problem, the reestablishment of the international circulation of goods and of capital remains an essential part of the whole situation.

This, then, is the series of measures to be taken, while recognizing and proclaiming that these measures constitute a totality, and that they can have their effects only if they reciprocally support each other—abolition of the hindrances to commerce, liberation and reorganization of the movements and of the transfers of capital, and finally, the reestablishment of an international monetary standard.

* * * * * *

1) The first part of the task will therefore consist in an attack upon the obstacles which block the international exchange of goods. It will be necessary to do away with the formal or surreptitious prohibitions, revise the provisions to that end, and change the spirit in which the customs administrations have hitherto worked.

It will then be necessary to give up the system of quotas and licenses. It will be necessary, especially, to reestablish, in international competition, the elementary rules of economic morality, and perhaps provide for sanctions to secure respect for them. And lastly, it will be necessary to lower the customs barriers.

Here the danger to be avoided is that of appearing too exacting, and of asking more than is strictly necessary.

In order that goods may begin to circulate again it is not indispensable that all customs tariffs should be forced down wholesale and without delay. It is necessary, and it is sufficient, to begin with, that increases be stopped; thereafter, adjustments can be made gradually. This adjustment should comprise several steps; what is essential is to regularize to some degree the incidence of tariffs upon the different products, or in other words, bring the various duties specified in the tariff into approximation to the total average rates, so as to avoid having certain articles assessed with duties so high as to amount to a prohibition. The purpose would also be served by simplifying the enumerations, and applying the rules of nomenclature proposed by the League of Nations. Conventions among groups of countries, allowing for the gradual lowering of tariffs, should be multiplied or extended; for this purpose, the Ouchy Convention might serve as a guide and as a precedent.

Such provisions as these would make it possible to achieve the purpose in view without sudden or useless overturns. They are not at all inconsistent with the maintenance of moderate tariffs, of a fiscal character, whose existence would not stand in the way of any essential movement.

2) The second part of the task will consist in rebuilding and setting again in motion the mechanism of the financing of international economy.

Here too, it is by an act of cleansing and of healing that a beginning must be made. We will not insist further upon the necessity of settling the question of war debts and of reparations; the boats will not begin to pass through the canal again, so long as this double log-boom obstructs it.

Just as in the case of goods it will be necessary, in order to reestablish the movement of international capital, to remove the principal obstacles in the way of its circulation. That means the ending of exchange regulations, clearing agreements, etc.

But such an opening of the gates can be imagined only if the past has been so dealt with as to keep it from unduly burdening the present.

Means must therefore be found to consolidate the arrears in one form or another, and to replace by definite agreements the temporary or incoherent or unilateral solutions with which we have had to content ourselves thus far.

Once the ground is cleared in this way, we will have to rebuild. But we need not be afraid; when the principal obstacles have disappeared, private initiative will be quite capable of filling the gaps, and taking back its old place.

Meanwhile, it will perhaps appear necessary to provide transitional organizations, and processes which will help to get the machinery again in gear—great public works, special funds, institutions for medium-term credit, state assistance in arranging guarantees, etc. Such proposals will of course have to be examined and judged each on its own merits.

It will also be important to make use of all the possibilities of the existing organizations (such, for example, as the Bank for International Settlements) though with such modifications as necessity or utility may show to be needed. In any case, there will have to be measures that succeed in creating,

11

in the field of credit, that atmosphere of security and ease which enterprise requires for its development. A policy of cheap money, and an ordered expansion of credit, will seem the more advisable and the more effective if supported by a policy of foregoing adventure and avoiding doubtful innovations in the monetary field.

3) But there will remain still a third portion, and a delicate one, of the task—the establishment of an international standard of values, which will once more give stability of exchange.

As for myself, it is my definite conviction that we should go back to the gold standard and that we will go back to it. From the practical point of view, there is no other choice possible. Whatever may be the theoretical merits of ingenious systems, there is no other which today presents the same political advantages, whether as a matter of the guarantees that it offers against certain temptations on the part of those in power, or because it is in fact the only one on which there is any chance of obtaining unanimity among the nations.

Most of the complaints that have been made against the gold standard, in recent years, have been ill-directed; they were really directed either against abuses of the rules necessary to the functioning of the gold standard, or against conditions of fact which went far beyond the realm of monetary influences, and were directely related either to politics or to the general economic situation. Under conditions involving such nationalistic withdrawal and isolation as have prevailed in the world, no international standard could persist at all— neither the gold standard nor any other.

It remains none the less true that mistakes have been committed within the proper domain of gold. They must be perceived and corrected and made impossible for the future; in other words the working rules of the gold standard must be defined anew.

Among such rules, there can be no escaping the necessity of giving a place anew to the gold exchange standard. It is in this, unquestionably, that the greatest mistakes have been made; it is in this that definitions, limitations and corrections will be the most necessary. But the task is not technically impossible. In an atmosphere of international good will, it would soon come to appear a very simple matter.

In the monetary field, there is one method which has already proved itself—that is the collaboration among banks of issue. Use should be made of it again. The gold standard, put back into an adequate framework, revivified in a world where goods and capital can circulate once more, reestablished in accordance with the rules which give it its international character and enable it to assure the maintenance of practical stability in exchange and in prices—under such conditions the gold standard will soon regain the favor that it so long enjoyed; and its reestablishment will complete the measures establishing on a firm basis the recovery for which we are hoping.

*   *   *   *   *   *

Confronting so vast and so drastic a programme, one can not avoid some feeling of uneasiness. Such advice has been so often given; there has so often been an attempt to follow it; and so often we have failed. Will we succeed better this time? It would be enough if we really wished it.

For a change has come about. The misery has become so widespread and so deep that everyone, without exception, is conscious today that something must be done. Many are prepared for sacrifices which a year ago would have seemed to them inconceivable.

There has been, moreover, an experiment carried out to the full—that by which the nations have tried to find in economic nationalism remedies for their ills. It has led them into a blind alley, and public opinion begins to realize the fact. There is an element of hope in this state of mind of the public. Leaving aside all academic discussions of the relative advantages of protectionism and free trade, many people are now ready to take an empirical attitude; since the method followed has only given bad results, let it be abandoned, and another be tried; no worse one can possibly be found, and it is almost a certainty that a better one can be.

To be sure, this programme has in it nothing original or beguiling. It calls for a great deal of courage and of perseverance, and involves giving up many illusions.

But, as was once said by Cardinal Mercier, the desire for originality is often a hindrance to truth.

We must not hide from ourselves, either, the extent of the task. All these points, each of which is essential, are bound together, and form a whole that must be treated as such.

What good would it do to abolish customs barriers if the obstacles to payment were allowed to remain? What good would it do to try to set the financial mechanism in motion, if goods were not exchanged? How could a system of international financing exist if it had not the support of a common and stable standard of value? And how, either, could an international standard function, without an economy that was effectively and practically international?

The same interdependence among the problems is evident also from the geographic point of view. We have seen how the peoples have been led, one after the other, and one because of the other, into the way of economic nationalism.

And now they have no way of getting rid of these artificial defenses that they have raised around themselves, except by a general plan and on the condition that each one does its part, and at the same time.

Let us add, too, even though it is not within the scope to which we had limited ourselves, that it will be necessary to consider means of reestablishing order in the conditions of production and use of certain of the great products such, for example, as wheat or copper or silver.

Indeed, as was said at Lausanne, the way of escape from the crisis must be found within the framework of a general settlement of all the problems involved. That is the work that awaits the International Economic Conference, which alone is able to undertake it with any chance of success.

But is not that too much to ask of it? We think not.

To begin with, that Conference will have been better prepared for than many others. The proposed agenda, which has been drawn up and annotated by the Geneva Preparatory Commission, unquestionably affords an excellent point of departure. Encouraging signs have been manifest even in the drafting of this project. The experts held two meetings for the purpose, one at the beginning of November, 1932, the other two months later. But between these two meetings, the atmosphere had completely changed; from being heavy and stifling, as it was at first, it had become confident and constructive; and by the end, there had come to exist a genuine spirit of international collaboration.

And there is, furthermore, some change in the United States. The persistent abstention of the most powerful state in the world had cast a shadow over the whole history of the period since the war. But today it seems that the United States has understood that its very importance makes impossible, in its own direct interests, a persistence in this negative attitude. It is for the United States to take the control levers in hand. If it adopts at the future conference a clear-cut and constructive course of action, it will certainly, and immediately, be followed first by the great European powers, and in the end by the great majority of peoples. The success of the Conference therefore depends principally upon the position that the United States may take. For my part, I cannot but see in this fact a considerable basis for hope.

And finally (let us say it clearly, to reassure the timid), although it is indispensable that the Conference should make a beginning towards the solution of these interrelated problems, it is not necessary that it should from the beginning go either very high or very deep in its work.

The crisis is very far along in its evolution; it has already, in spite of everything, had a large proportion of its customary consequences; many of the weak have been sacrificed; many excesses have been corrected by force of circumstances; many accumulations of goods have been consumed or at least reduced; many efforts towards healing and towards adaptation to new conditions have been made everywhere. Barring new and grave events, which it depends upon us to avoid, it may be said that we have passed the period of decline and entered into that of the depression properly so called. The natural elements of the case are therefore ready to respond to the touch that would put them again on the way towards adjustment.

At this point in the crisis, reactions of a psychological sort may work favorably, with a double influence. If the world were, for the first time, to find before it a series of simple but essential decisions, forming a whole, and definitely attacking the problem from the right angle, there can be no doubt that the moral effect would be enormous and would have far-reaching consequences; and this time, the appeal to confidence would be legitimate and effective because it would be based upon a realistic policy, and not merely upon appearances.

It would be enough if the Conference were merely to go as far as it reasonably can in its work of clearing and dis-encumbering the world of the largest of the obstacles; then the stream would begin to flow again, by itself—slowly at first, but soon more vigorously. As soon as the touch has been given, and we have got out of the vicious circle in which we are spinning (and in which a decline leads to another decline, a restriction to a greater restriction, and a misery to a vaster misery), there might be a complete reversal; whatever caused pressure in the wrong direction would now lend its weight on the other side of the balance. Little by little—more quickly, doubtless, than we dare to hope—we would achieve a degree of order, a level of prices, and a volume of work, which would allow humanity to begin again living with respect for contracts, with dignity in the wages earned, and with social peace.

Let us hope that we will not exceed this point of equilibrium so madly as we did before. We will then have to be careful to avoid a relapse into the mistakes of prosperity, and to assure a sufficient stability of prices, of business, of active purchasing power, and of social relationships. But worries on that score must still seem to us like chimeras, or like sirens. We can promise them a welcome when they really come.

*   *   *   *   *   *

Now, if the Conference realizes only a part of the hopes we have based upon it, it will be said to have achieved a great—a very great—success.

However, we cannot but realize that the real problem— the essential one—is still vaster and graver; its complete

solution does not belong to any conference, however powerful or however successful it may be.

The organization, or the reorganization, of international
economic life, under the new conditions arising out of technical progress and economic developments, puts in the foreground the very problem of the organization or reorganization
of political relations themselves.

There is growing and spreading, among larger and larger
groups, the impression that the methods and the organisms,
through which these political relations are carried on, are
unadapted, or imperfectly adapted, to the new conditions of
the economic life of the world. Surely, the crisis has given
considerable clearness and emphasis to that opinion. But the
question will not cease to exist, once the crisis has passed.
The answer to it must be found, if we are to avoid in the
future a return of the miseries from which we are suffering
today. In any case, and at any price, we must find means of
avoiding for the future having the international economic
order overturned by uncoordinated efforts along national
lines—efforts which do no good to anyone, and are hurtful
to all.

So the organization of international life in all its aspects—
not only economic, but also and more particularly political—
will for long remain one of the primary concerns of the best
minds on either side of the ocean. The stake at issue is no
less than our civilization itself. I will cite, in concluding,
only one testimony — that of the Geneva experts in their
report drawn up for the use of the coming world conference.
This is their warning, moderate but solemn:

Such a choice [that is, a choice other than that of economic dis-
armament] would shake to its foundations the international financial structure; the standards of living would go down, and the social
system which we know could scarcely survive. These results, if they
were to come about, could not be imputed to any inescapable natural
law, but to the failure of human will and intelligence, proving themselves incapable of putting into effect the necessary international
guarantees along political and economic lines.

April 15, 1933.